PRE-VACCINATION PUPPY TRAINING

a sure-start guide
for
you and your puppy

Julie Hindle

Pre-Vaccination Puppy Training

ISBN–13: 978-1530197798

ISBN–10: 1530197791

Published by Abelenus Press 2016

Maidenhead, England

Cover Photograph (Cover Girl Laika) © 2016 Julie Hindle

Photo credits

All photographs and line drawings © Julie Hindle except for

© Krista Guziolek–pages 93, 11, 112,144
   and photo 1 on page 110, photo 6 on page 113

© Nate Hindle Photography–pages 12, 18, 121

© Ashley Paton Photography–pages 31, 64, 108, 140

© Nicolette Tracey–pages 53, 57, 59, 62, 63

© Vicky Wilkins–page 27

Table of Contents

Acknowledgements

If it were possible, I would thank each and every dog I have had the pleasure to live and work with individually. They gave me the opportunity to gain the experience and the tools I needed to make life better for all the dogs that came after them.

I would also like to say a huge thank you to John and Jennifer Whitfield for taking a chance on me many years ago when I turned up at *Warley and District Dog Training Club (Birmingham),* and said that I wanted to be a dog trainer. Even though I had no dog at the time! What a strange, young-person I must have seemed to you both.

Thank you to my husband for helping to produce this book.

Finally, to my pack of **'Clever Canines'** who I currently share my home with, they are truly amazing. They share my attention without ever a cross-word with each other and tolerate all that I ask from them. They are forever forgiving of me, even when I get it wrong. I love each and every one of them for their uniqueness in the challenge, company and fun they offer me. **You are simply the best!**

| Twyla | Bettie | Mosi |
| Amara | Laika | Beanie |

Why I wrote this book

The aim of this book is to provide you with everything you need to create a stress-free environment for you, your family, and your puppy. Pre-vaccination training covers around three to four weeks—from the day you collect your pup until she has completed her vaccinations and can go walking in public.

Three weeks or so may not seem like a long time to you, but it is a crucial period in a pup's early development. These first few weeks can make the difference between having an insecure pup (for example, being needy, lead-reactive, crying in the night) and a pup that is confident in dealing with everyday situations.

I've worked with owners and their dogs since the mid-1980s. Many owners brought their pups to my training classes with problems that had developed during the few weeks that their pups were confined to home in the initial vaccination period. I discovered that the pups had received little to no training during this time. Problem behaviours such as toileting, play-biting, growling when told 'No!', and being overly timid or nervous could have been prevented if their owners had started to train their pup the moment it came into the home.

To be fair, this wasn't the fault of the owners. The conventional wisdom at the time was that training for a puppy started at six months. Unfortunately, the conventional wisdom in this instance was wrong! By the time a puppy is six months old its basic character and behaviours are well on their way to being formed.

During the late 1980s, I undertook some applied research into working with owners and their pups in their homes during the initial vaccination stage—the results were amazing! I then designed a training programme for owners to train their pups as soon as the pups entered their new homes. I would make a one-off visit to see the owner and their pup to explain and demonstrate my training

8

programme. And so, my 'Pre-Vaccination Puppy-Training' programme was born.

This is the first time that I've written the details of my programme in a book—it's the nearest thing to a home visit from me, and much more. By following this programme, you are being proactive in preventing bad habits forming in the early days. It is my hope that in reading this book you will:

> Feel supported and assured that I am right alongside you, guiding you through the most important part of your journey with your new pup.
> Prevent mistakes from happening by getting a head-start on shaping the pup that you want to share your home and life.
> Provide a stress-free environment for your pup, allowing you to bond and enjoy her without regretting your decision to bring a pup into your home.

Throughout the book, I will refer to your dog as 'she', (unless the context is gender specific) for no other reason than all my dogs are she's and therefore I will use what comes more naturally to me.

Welcome to pre-vaccination puppy training and thank you for allowing me to be part of your journey.

I would love to hear how you get on with your training, after reading the book. Please feel free to email me at **julie@acek9.net** and send me your comments.

01 Pre-Vaccination Puppy Training

In this chapter
- What is pre-vaccination training?
- When should training start?
- What type of training is a puppy capable of at this early age?

What is pre-vaccination training?

Pre-vaccination, is the time before your puppy has finished her vaccination programme, for most pups this will be around thirteen weeks old mark. Your pup is as capable of learning during this time as she will be as an adult dog. The main difference will be her physical capabilities; she will have already started to develop a relationship with you and your family through this period.

Training during the pre-vaccination period will give your pup the best possible start towards becoming a balanced dog, a great family member, and a dog that fits into society. During this period:

- Your pup is at the most impressionable time in her life.
- Your pup has a natural follow-the-leader instinct. You need to be tapping into this time, it will make recall training so much easier. *See chapter 13 for Recall training.*
- You and your family need to bond with your pup, so that she looks to you for direction and leadership.
- You need to establish good habits in your pup, to avoid unwanted bad habits developing later on.

Most problems of socialising arise during this time. Veterinary advice, quite rightly, dictates that your pup should not socialise with other pups or dogs until one week after their final vaccination, this could mean thirteen or fourteen weeks of age, depending upon the age you purchase your puppy and your vet's vaccination programme. This could also mean that your pup's most critical socialisation period has passed (between eight to thirteen weeks), this can mean the difference between a nervous, insecure puppy and a well-adjusted socially acceptable dog.

Although your pup may not be allowed out to run and socialise, there are a number of steps you can take in the right direction to enable training and socialisation to take place. This early period is very valuable and an important time that should not be wasted.

When should training start?
Many owners feel that they have plenty of time before needing to begin their training, some, may not even think about training until, they discover they have a problem.

For many, many years the general opinion was that six-months of age was time enough to begin training. Fortunately, we have left that opinion in the distant past. Waiting until a pup is six-months old means that you would have let the most important part of your dog's development go by without having had any influence on the behaviour patterns which will influence the rest of your life together.

By the age of six-months your dog may have established independence and some issues that may prove difficult to break through. Getting her attention and getting her to focus on you, will prove harder and there may be no connection between you or your family and your dog.

Hormones also begin to play a big part in your dog's character make-up, by the time many are six-months old, particularly in small to medium size breeds, (different dogs develop and mature at different rates). This could mean problems ahead for you and your dog. It is at this point that the owner usually seeks help from trainers and behaviourists, potentially ending up spending a fortune on trying to reform their now difficult or so called delinquent dog. In my experience, Pre-vaccination Puppy Training, prevents, these problems from the outset.

What type of training is a puppy capable of at this early age?

Early training is based upon the domestic dog's wild ancestors. When a litter of pups is born in the wild, the mother doesn't wait until the pups are six-months before she decides to teach them how to hunt, or where they belong within the pack. The pups would die very quickly if left to act on their own initiative for this length of time. The pups would also wreak havoc if they didn't learn the rules, structure and boundaries within the pack!

Learning what their role is within the family creates harmony and safety and stops problems from arising. It is your job, as the new pack-leader to follow on from where your pup's mum, littermates and the breeder left off, this is key for developing a contented, confident, happy, and well-balanced dog.

One of my Litters being whistle trained and learning not to jump up for food, before going to their new homes.

All good manners need to be put in place now! Do not wait until your puppy is six-months or one-year old to assume the role of their leader. Stepping up to the role from the moment they enter your home, helps your puppy to know who runs the home, who the home belongs to and where she fits in, this creates a relaxed contented pup and a peaceful family environment.

It is important that you are consistent and, contrary to popular belief, dogs are more stressed when left to do their own thing and given the freedom to go wherever they want. They need structure and order to function and to remain balanced. If you don't provide this, be certain that your dog **will** provide it for you, she will develop her own rules and boundaries and this is when problems start to creep in for you and your family.

Your pup is as capable of learning now as it will be as an adult. Here are some of the good behaviours that your pup is capable of learning from the minute she enters your home.

Good Boundaries
- Where she sleeps.
- Where and when she is allowed to toilet.
- Which rooms and locations in the house are out of bounds.

And yes, there should be some 'No Go' areas, that are for you and your 'human' family only at this stage in your relationship with your pup. At the very least, until she can be trusted with freedom and knows the house rules.

Good Manners
- No rushing through doorways.
- No charging through the house going wherever she wants to.
- No jumping on the furniture including your beds etc.
- No biting or mouthing.
- No jumping up.
- Food manners i.e., no possessiveness, remaining calm while food is being made and presented to her.
- Grooming routine.

Basic Training
Then there's the basic training that we humans like our dogs to know.
- Sit
- Down
- Stand
- Wait
- Stay
- Leave
- Come, when called
- Walking without pulling on a lead

02 Understanding your Dog

In this chapter
- Behavioural matters
- What is a normal puppy?
- Does your dog really need a pack?
- Role-play
- What makes a good leader?

Behavioural matters

Understanding the basics of dog behaviour is essential if you are to have a happy dog who gets on and fits into your world.

I would highly recommend that you purchase a good book or DVD on dog behaviour, there is also lots of information available on the internet, but make sure you go to a reputable source. The Kennel Club can be a good place to find suitable information on dog training and breeds etc. **www.thekennelclub.org.uk**

Learning about dogs in general, will help you understand why they do the things they do and so, aid you in your training. Dog behaviour applies to all dogs irrespective of the breed. It is crucial that you understand your dog's language, before trying to get her to understand yours. Canine language is made up of signs and signals given through body gestures and verbal sounds. Understanding what your dog is telling you and how she is feeling, is important so that you both understand each other. This will help build a relationship of trust and respect.

Did you know that when your dog yawns, it can mean she is tired but it can also mean she is feeling stressed and under pressure? Your dog will tell you when she's happy and comfortable, by how she wags her tail and greets people, but her tail can also be an indication that she is frightened, dominant, or unsure of the situation. Your dog will bark and howl to alert you that someone is approaching your house. She may also bark and howl to tell you that she wants her family back home when she is left home alone, and bark when she is excited to be going out or that you have returned home. It is important to learn what she is telling you.

Different breeds of dogs may vary in some of the behaviour traits and temperaments they exhibit. Learning about the characteristics of your breed and why they do the things they do, will endear you more to your dog and you will learn to embrace your dog's whole character rather than trying to work against it. So, it is hardly surprising that if you choose a Terrier, that they want to dig holes in your garden—the name Terrier means to go to ground. Terriers are bred to hunt mice, rats, rabbits etc. Perhaps your Newfoundland can't resist sitting in his water bowl, they are after all, a water rescue dog!

Understanding what your dog was bred for will help you to be more tolerant and sympathetic to your dog. This will also aid you in your training to harness your dog's particular traits. So when your Tibetan Terrier is trying to climb to the highest lookout point, it will come as no surprise to you when they take over the window ledge or book case to  look out the window or climb a tree to see over the neighbour's fence to scan their territory for intruders, they were after all bred as alert dogs in the monasteries.

However, whatever your breed, this doesn't mean they have to do these things written in their history book. You just need to be aware of them and to learn to shape the behaviour to what you would prefer them to do. It is also good to remember, a dog is a dog first and a breed second. Do not get hung up on what your dog can and can't do, or should and shouldn't do 'as a breed'. This will get in the way of helping your dog to reach her full potential.

What is a normal puppy?
Never assume that because you have a well-behaved puppy that they will grow up to be a well-behaved dog. There is no evidence to support this, in fact in my experience it is often quite the contrary.

A well-behaved puppy can quite often have hidden problems that only come to light as the puppy gains its confidence or as it grows and matures. So take comfort, if you feel you have a very naughty puppy, at least 'what you see is what you get' and you can shape the behaviour to suit your lifestyle.

A 'normal' puppy, if there is such a thing, runs around manic at times. They all do it, the mad-half hour or the *zoomies*, you will become familiar with these terms once you own a dog for a while. The normal puppy is into everything—eyes in the back of your head springs to mind.

They should have a natural inquisitive nature, grabbing at anything in their path, and at times even you. Their general pattern is eat, sleep, play, wee and poo and somewhere in between, all of those other behaviours. If this sounds like the puppy in your life, then congratulations, you are the proud owner of a normal healthy pup.

Of course there is always the exception to the rule, you may get lucky and have a well-behaved puppy, and she may turn into a well-behaved adult, relatively trouble free, but I can assure you this is the exception, rather than the rule. Keep in mind at all times that whatever behaviours your puppy exhibits, whether you like them or not, the chances are she is just being a dog. She will have no concept that the behaviour is wrong or annoying or not called for. Your dog is not doing it to spite you and neither is she out to get you. She is simply being the only thing she knows how to be—a dog.

Does your dog really need a pack?

She may have started out as a pack-animal, but being the adaptable animal she is, we know that she can learn to live as an individual, as many stray or street dogs do. They don't crumple and die if they haven't got a pack around them. However, the key is this, put her back into a pack situation and she will look for structure, order and balance in order to function.

It does not matter whether it is within a canine (dog) pack, or as part of a human pack this is of no significance to the dog, as long as there is an order that is clear to follow. It is important from the beginning to remember that a dog will always be a dog; it is not a child or a human. If you do not keep order and boundaries in place for your dog, things will go wrong. It doesn't matter how much of a 'friend' you want to be to your dog, the best friend you can be is the one who guides and leads the way. Leaving them to their own devices will not create a happy, balanced dog who wants to be with you and listen to you. If you do not provide this structure and you leave your dog to make her own choices and decisions, cracks begin to appear in the system, and soon the relationship will start to break down and problems will become very apparent.

Remember that your pup has been removed from her mum and litter-mates, to live with you. You have now become her family and her pack. If you aren't prepared to establish an order, rest assured your pup will do it for you.

Fortunately, being a pack-animal by nature, gives her a desire to be cooperative and adaptive, with a willingness to please. It is this very instinct which has made the dog such an adaptable and acceptable companion, she thrives on human company and working alongside us.

Within every pack a strong sense of order is maintained, through instructions and structure, which creates balance for each member, each one having a role to play. For many years this has been known as the "pecking order". However, in current times many trainers and behaviourists prefer to think of this as a *team* and a family working together. Irrespective of how you view it, your dog needs leadership to guide her, so that she learns where she fits in and what her role is within the team or pack. It is irrelevant to the dog whether the leader is male or female. Within a pack of dogs sometimes there are both genders at the head of the pack.

17

Role-play

Pups are taught to hunt during play sessions; they also begin to learn where they fit in within their canine pack from the day they are born. They learn by pushing and shoving their way to the best milk supply from their mum and they jostle to have the best sleeping place. This is an ongoing process as they grow and gain strength, constantly wrestling to find their position in their pack and litter. They learn also to respect the adult members of the wider pack from the moment they leave the Den. This is why it is so important that we take on the responsibility and role of the mother when a pup enters our world. We need to equip the pup with the rules and order she needs to fit into our social structure.

What makes a good leader?

A good canine and human leader leads with calmness, and confident control. A good leader, sets rules and instructions that are given through strong clear signs and signals.

The team (or pack) work closely together, and remain very loyal to each other giving protection and support. The leader will say what happens and what does not within the team, keeping everyone in line to maintain order and harmony. A good leader does not need to use excessive force and they never lose their temper. They would be seen as unpredictable and respect would be lost if they displayed outbursts of temper.

It is because of this natural desire to be led, that dogs are keen to take instructions and accept the training and guidelines that we set for them so readily. Contrary to what some dog owners feel, most dogs which are allowed to do what they want on a day-to-day basis are not happy dogs and quite often display signs of frustration and discontentment within the home and outside.

Being your dog's leader is essential for your dog to remain balanced, trustworthy and respectful, don't let her down.

03 Before your Puppy Arrives

Time to puppy-proof your home and garden

So you have chosen to open up your home to a puppy. How exciting! But, did you know that there are a number of steps you should take to puppy-proof your home and garden? Don't leave it to chance and hope that everything will be fine. A thorough check should be carried out both inside and outside of your home.

Ensuring that your home is a safe environment for a puppy is essential as a responsible pet owner. There are many potentially dangerous hazards that need to be removed or made safe for your pup, preferably before she arrives. Puppy-proofing your home is pretty much like baby-proofing before the arrival of a child, although you get more time to do this with a baby than with a puppy.

With a pup, the safety check needs to be a little more extreme before he or she arrives, than with a baby. Pups are much more curious, mobile, capable and more destructive from the beginning. They will investigate and test things much earlier than a baby ever will. Pups test things using their mouths and paws. This can lead them into serious trouble.

Pups (just like babies and toddlers) have no sense of danger, they have no concept what is safe and what is not. They will pick up, touch and knock anything and everything they can get access too. Unfortunately some dogs never grow out of this curious nature, and if you are unlucky they never learn and will always prove hazardous to themselves. It is worth keeping this in mind and always ensure that precautions are taken with potentially dangerous areas or products unless you can guarantee that your dog's curiosity will not get the better of her.

This chapter is dedicated to giving you a comprehensive guide of helpful tips, to keep your puppy safe and free from trouble. Where possible, it is best to take these precautions before bringing your new pup into your home.

What is puppy-proofing?

A lot of what we are talking about here is common sense, but sometimes we forget; sometimes the obvious just misses our attention, particularly when a new pup is imminent, as the anticipation and excitement of a new puppy can cloud our judgement. Puppy-proofing is about viewing your home and garden from your pup's point of view—walking in their paws in order to anticipate and prevent any possible dangerous situations from ever happening.

Puppy-proofing avoids situations where pups need telling off, or correcting constantly. This means you spend far more time enjoying your pup's company and your pup gets to enjoy you. Pups thrive on positivity, always keep this in mind. If you are constantly telling your pup off, this positive learning experience will be missed.

Puppy-proofing is protecting your home and your possessions and your pup. Everything is a potential toy to your pup and is fair game to her, but to you some things are precious. She does not understand what valuables are and what is precious to you. Puppy-proofing prevents damage which can cause thousands of pounds and prevents potential ill-health for your puppy.

How to puppy-proof your home

If you allow your pup access to something, she will assume it is hers to get her teeth into. She will have no concept of 'don't touch', or 'it's not yours'. The thing I find the most frustrating is when people say, 'She should know it's not hers and she mustn't touch it'. How should she know that? Because you told her? She's a dog, and has no concept of the value of your glasses, the TV remote, your wallet or purse, or the table leg.

Mr Tibs' Training Tip

*What you consider valuable, I can guarantee you, your pup will
not, I didn't. Everything is up for grabs if you
allow your pup access to it.*

1. You need to protect your belongings from
   puppy teeth and paws and prevent
   unwanted behaviours from developing.
   'Prevention is always better than cure'.
2. If you value it, move it. Especially, if you are not around to teach
   her not to touch it.
3. If it's dangerous or expensive, they won't care because they have
   no concept of monetary value or danger.
4. Pups should not be free to wander around your house. You
   wouldn't leave your toddler to wander alone, neither should
   your pup. Disasters can happen in a second.
5. Close supervision at all times is essential for your pup's
   wellbeing.
6. Confine your pup to a small, secure room, a puppy pen or,
   consider crate-den training to help prevent accidents from
   happening and teach your puppy her place within the home.
7. Keeping your pup restricted when you are not available to watch
   her, is always a better option than trying to solve the problem,
   once it has been allowed to start, and it also proves to be much
   cheaper.
8. Chew toys should be available at all times. What 'you' consider a
   suitable chew toy, your pup may not. Make sure you have tried
   and tested chew toys with your pup and they are worth the effort
   of chewing on to her.

Toys – Will keep your puppy occupied, help with teething, and
alleviate the stress of boredom. Many dogs need to be taught to play
or chew on the right thing.

Make sure you have a good selection of toys and vary them, daily.
Toys often lose their appeal and value, if puppy sees them all the
time, variety is good.

Many dogs prefer to chew wood or plastic, and some may even get a passion for plaster or concrete, it is your job to teach them that these are not acceptable materials to chew on. You cannot do this if you are not there, so make sure she is in a secure location when you are out of the room and you are unable to monitor her desires. Dogs are a creature of habit, if they never get to do something as a puppy, the likelihood is they will not do it as an adult, off course there is always the exception to the rule.

There are many items on the market as a deterrent for chewing on things. Bitter-tasting sprays that may deter dogs from chewing on items that cannot possibly be moved. e.g. table legs, skirting boards and corners of cabinets can be saved in this way, although this may need a little trial and error, as some dogs are not even deterred by these and may even be quite partial to them.

Plants and poisons

Indoor plants: A good idea is to list the types of plants you have in your house. If you are not sure, take photos of them and check them online or at a garden centre. There is always someone who knows and only too willing to pass on their knowledge and information.

Here is a basic list of the most common house and garden plants that are poisonous to your dog. This is not a comprehensive list, so please check for others.

Amaryllis bulbs, asparagus fern, azalea, cyclamen, daffodil bulbs, daylilies, delphiniums, foxgloves, hemlock, hyacinth, hydrangea, ivy, laburnum, lilies, lily of the valley, lupins, mistletoe, morning glory, nightshade, oleander, poinsettia, rhododendron, rhubarb leaves, sweet pea, tulip bulbs, umbrella plant, wisteria, yew and some berries, mushrooms and toadstools

If your dog chews or eats any of these, seek veterinary help immediately.

Hazards and poisons: Make sure anything potentially poisonous is securely locked away or stored high and out of reach. Did you know that one of the most common household killers in both cats and dogs is Antifreeze? Your pet can equally die from licking this from the roadside where cars have been parked. Do not let them drink from street puddles. Many pets are attracted to antifreeze due to the sweet aroma it emits.

Other common hazards are: Household cleaners, rat poisons, mothballs, insect repellents, bleaches, disinfectants, insecticides, pesticides, soaps, shampoos and laundry detergents. Again this is by no means a comprehensive list.

Remember if your pup ingests any item that she shouldn't, your first action should be to **call the vet** and your second action after dealing with it is, give yourself a good talking to. Don't get angry with your pup, she was only being the only thing she knows how to be, a puppy or dog. All anger should lay at your feet for not doing that which was preventable.

A pup's eye view

Try to think like a puppy, as silly as it sounds it may even be worth getting down on your hands and knees in each room of your home and look for possible attractions that a puppy might see! Friends and family may laugh at you, but the last laugh will be yours when you save your pup's life.

Never assume that pups won't be interested in something. Trust me they will. If it sticks out, they will pull it off, if it moves they will chase it, if they can get their head in it, you can guarantee they will—and then probably, will not be able to pull it back out again!

Start at the entrance to each room, and work your way around it, check all furniture, wall, sockets, wires, cables, are there doors they can open? Drawers they could get into? Curtain cords dangling, curtains they can swing on. Items left lying around? Plastic bags etc.

Things they can climb up on, to reach other things and perhaps fall off. Regard nothing as safe and everything as fair game in your pup's mind. Falling is a big reality and bones do break. Getting up is always easier than getting down for a puppy, so don't let her climb.

If you have children, now is a good time to encourage them with your help, to sort their toys and make sure there are boxes with lids for everything. Many pups will swallow anything that can go down.

Everyday hazards for pups

Small items:
- Remove and store out of reach, coins, paper clips, children's toys, jewellery, small ornaments, and tissues.
- Laundry – socks and underwear are firm favourites. Many socks have been removed from the intestines of puppies. Believe me, what goes in, doesn't always come out.

Larger items:
- Wallets and purses, mobile phones. Everything must be placed out of reach. Not only are these frustrating to lose but are often expensive to replace and many of these items may contain toxic elements for your pup such as batteries or magnets.
- If it's on the floor your pup will assume it is there for her to have. Your best leather shoes or trainers make excellent chew toys to a pup, and they are always a firm favourite—leather is great for cutting their teeth on.
- Pups cannot distinguish between their chew toy and your expensive shoes, at least not in the early days.

Rubbish bins:
- I wish I had a pound for every time some asks me, 'How do I stop my dog from stealing'? My answer: don't let it start in the first place! You guessed it, 'Prevention is better than cure'.
- When choosing a bin, aim for a type that your pup cannot get into, or lock your bins away in cupboards that they can't access. Eating trash is a habit you really need to prevent from ever starting. Pups swallowing packaging is a real health hazard and

you'll be forever cleaning up after them if they form this habit. Stealing is one of the hardest behaviours to solve, purely because it is self-rewarding. They see it, they eat it, they enjoy it! There is no correction after the fact that will take away that enjoyment of consuming their find, even if they vomit, they don't associate it was because of what they ate.

- Never leave any food out where your puppy may get it. Many human foods are toxic to dogs and others are just plain unhealthy due to high fat and sugar content. There's also the chance that your pup could choke on packaging or string.

- Some particularly hazardous foods are: cooked bones, no matter what type; chocolate; coffee granules; tea bags; onions; grapes and raisins; and many more besides. To be safe, try to put all food away immediately, removing all temptation and risk. Repeated scavenging can lead to serious health problems such as pancreatitis due to the body's inability to process extreme changes in diet such as fatty foods.

Around the house

Chewing hazards

- **Electrical wires** – are a huge hazard for chew-happy pups for very obvious reasons! You should do your very best to run cables out of your puppy's reach, run them through cable wraps or PVC tubing, spray them with bitter chew deterrents and unplug all electrical items when they aren't being used.

- **Furniture** - Treat all corners of furniture, skirting boards, lower half of walls and all doors with a bitter-tasting chew deterrent, at the first sign of your pup showing an interest. A lot of damage can be done in a short space of time when your back is turned.

- **Laundry** - Make sure all laundry and clothing is well out of reach. Worn clothes carry your smell, they're particularly appealing to your pup and swallowed socks or other items can easily cause intestinal blockages.

- **Medicines** - Make sure your pup can't get access to any medication, supplements or household cleaners. Pups make short work of getting into bottles and plastic containers and the contents could potentially be fatal. Child-proof safety latches are a really good idea on drawers, cabinet doors and your fridge, if your pup has general access to these places.

- I have had dogs all my life and until this year I have never had one I would have considered a hazardous pup. My current youngster is fascinated by smells, she is drawn with a strange fascination to anything that smells different and takes great pleasure in seeking them out. She took a bottle of bleach that I have always kept in the same location with all my dogs and chewed into it ingesting some of it and then promptly vomiting it back up. Fortunately, no lasting damage was done. Needless to say nothing is canine reachable in our home now and everything is battened down. I really was one of those people who thought, 'it will never happen to me, my dogs would never do that'. I never say 'never' now!

- **Flooring** - If possible, keep your pup in areas with flooring that they cannot chew and that are easy to clean. Rugs and carpets are easily destroyed by a pup, so if you cannot supervise them, keep them on tiled, wooden or linoleum flooring until they're house trained and are trusted not to chew.

Climbing, crawling, pulling hazards

- Make sure there are no heavy items that your pup could pull off a high surface. This means not leaving a tablecloth, that can be pulled and checking shelves and surfaces don't have a protruding edge that can be pulled on.

- All cords or string on blinds and curtains must be tied up out of reach. Pups love to play with these but they're a choke and strangulation risk.

- Take extra care of things like folding sofas or doors that slam shut in the wind. Your puppy may crawl under sofa beds so check they're clear before operating the mechanics. And for doors that slam in the wind, they can easily physically hurt your puppy if their leg or tail gets shut in it. So install self-closing door hinges if possible.

How to puppy-proof the yard or garden

Similar to puppy-proofing indoors, you need to make sure your garden contains nothing a pup can chew on, swallow, or destroy anything you have of value, but I'm not going to ask you to crawl around the garden on your hands and knees! Here is a list of general tips for puppy-proofing your outside areas to keep puppy and your belongings safe.

Firstly, if you have a large garden, I suggest that you create a smaller area, for your pup to remain restricted to for toilet training. (See Chapter 8 Toilet Training for details on creating a space)

Securing the boundary

• Your pup should be supervised at all times outdoors.
• Your fence - Make sure your fences are high enough to prevent her from getting over it as an adult. 6 foot is the recommended height. Do not encourage your puppy to jump on and off things and over things, this may help with jumping being low on her radar. Of course as usual, there is always the exception to the rule.
• Walk the entire fence-line to look for any holes or broken areas your puppy may squeeze through. They can get through smaller gaps than you may think, so be sure to make the perimeter secure, perhaps by using extra panels or chicken wire where areas look weak. Concrete or paving stones for gaps under fences are a good solution.
• Any puppy may try to escape the yard or garden by bolting through an open gate, install self-closing hinges on all gates or perhaps even proper locks. People often leave gates open, particularly children and forgetful delivery drivers, so self-closing or lockable gates that only family members can open are a real safety net.
• Also check the fence-line for any protruding screws, nails or wire that puppy could cut or impale themselves on.

- If you have a raised deck or balcony with a guard fence, you have to make sure the gaps are small enough to prevent your puppy from slipping through. Puppies can get through surprisingly small gaps so I would recommend installing chicken wire to completely block any ability to get through it, until they have grown large enough when you can remove it. You cannot be too careful with such things.
- You should also remember that many dogs are great at jumping, a grid or barrier along the balcony is essential to prevent a disaster from happening should your puppy decide to attempt jumping up.

Fertilizers and other consuming hazards

- If you use any poisons for pest control you must store these completely out of reach as previously mentioned and when you use them, restrict your puppy from the area until the poison is removed or dissipates.
- If you have a lawn or planted areas and use fertilizers, insecticides or pesticides, then you absolutely must make sure the ones you use are labelled as 'pet safe' or switch to organic and chemical free gardening.
- Just like your houseplants, check your garden plants against a list of known plants toxic to dogs and have these removed entirely, it will save a lot of stress. Pups really don't discriminate, they just grab and eat.
- Make sure all trash, and compost if you make it, is securely stored in puppy-proof containers as both can contain dangerous and toxic materials if consumed.

Hide-outs and water

If you have a shed, make sure your pup cannot crawl under it.

- Garden heaters, fire pits and BBQs pose an obvious risk due to fire and heat so make sure to keep puppy well away from these when in use, they will be drawn to them by smell and the desire to dig or role.
- Be sure to safely store away all your garden tools which are an obvious risk and very sharp hazard to a playful pup.

- If you have a pond or swimming pool, it's a good idea to fence this off until your pup has grown and proven a strong swimmer. Young pups can and do get into trouble with water.
- Make sure there are no electrical wires or water hoses that your pup can find and chew on. You will have to block access to them, bury them, or otherwise run them out of reach.

You're on the home stretch now

The goal of puppy-proofing is essentially protection of your pup and your property, because one thing's for sure: If there's trouble to be found, you can be sure that your puppy's going to find it!

Pups are mischievous by nature and can get themselves into all sorts of trouble. It's your responsibility to do the best you can to keep them safe inside and outside your home.

By taking the time to puppy-proof your home and make sure the whole family are meticulous with cleaning up after themselves, you'll give your pup the best and safest start in life.

It might seem like a lot of work at first, but once you've swept through your home and puppy-proofed it to a high level, it's not at all hard to keep up.

Remember it isn't forever! As your pup grows and matures and gets over the experimental and chew-heavy adolescent stage, and learn how to behave and prove that they know what they can and cannot chew on, you can start to relax the rules.

However, until they have fully proven they can be trusted, you should follow the old saying 'Prevention is better than cure' (that's the last time, I promise).

You have done a great thing in taking these steps and working through this section.

Following the guidelines in this book to make your home and garden a safe environment for your pup tells me that you will be a wonderful dog owner who is thoughtful and caring about the well-being of your pup. Your pup is lucky to be entering your safe world.

I hope you feel armed and prepared after completing your puppy-proofing. You can now look forward to the enjoyment of welcoming your new pup to your safe home environment.

04 Collecting your Pup – Are You Ready?

In this chapter

Before your pup arrives

You have made your home safe, but there are some additional essentials that need to be put in place before your pup arrives. It is vital that you have given thought to each of the above categories if your pup's transition into your home is to go smoothly. Waiting until your pup arrives before sorting such matters is a mistake. Things can quickly become chaotic and unsettling for you and your puppy, she needs to know where she fits in and what the rules and boundaries are from day one, which is the sole purpose for this book.

It is no good allowing her freedom to do whatever she wants and go wherever she chooses and then deciding to change things because she is weeing everywhere and chewing everything in her path. You will create strong protests from your pup if this happens, and confusion will set in.

Did I mention, dogs are creatures of habit? they like consistency and thrive on knowing where exactly they belong and fit in.

Sleeping arrangements

Where is your pup's sleeping place going to be? Your pup needs a small, quiet area. Common choices are Kitchen, Laundry-Utility room or a corner of the living room.

It is not a good idea to have multiple beds in various rooms. This very quickly creates a need for your pup to sleep in your company all of the time. Although in the early days having her by your bed at night in her crate-den is a good idea.

Within a week or two, your pup should be back in the kitchen or another room to avoid creating dependency and other problems later on, this is explained further in chapter 6, *Den Training.*

A small area also means you can restrict your puppy's mess, which makes cleaning easier. Prepare this area for your puppies arrival by cleaning well, removing any wires or other items the pup may chew, remove ornaments or anything the pup may bump into, remove anything from this area you don't want soiled, chewed or scratched and remove anything your pup may jump onto. Broken bones are a common hazard at this age from inquisitive pups. Getting up onto objects is one thing, but getting down again is always harder. *See the 'puppy proofing' section in chapter 3 – Before Your Puppy Arrives, for full detail.*

Chew time

Give your pup plenty of 'suitable' chew toys. Pups need to chew; it is what they do. So always provide an alternative for her or she will target the items you don't want her too.

Suitable toys are tough chew toys especially made for puppies. Rope toys are great for chewing on and *Kongs* are great for stuffing with treats and meaty paste. *See chapter 14 – for photos and details of toys.*

- It is a good idea to have a toy box to store your pup's toys in.
- Don't let her have them all at once.
- Rotate the toys each day. Pups get bored quickly, if she sees the same toys every minute of every day, she will transfer her

attention to other more exciting things that don't belong to her, like table and chair legs, or door frames.

Collars and leads

A puppy collar and lead, nothing too heavy and steer clear of chain leads, these are never a good choice. My preferred choice for a puppy collar is a normal leather one or material buckle collar [see Photo 1].

Photo 1

I don't like the snap together ones although they are the most common at the moment. I have seen too many come apart under pressure. Remember to check your pup's collar regularly as puppies grow at an alarming rate and the collar must not become too tight.

Photo 2

If you have chosen a long-haired breed, I suggest you consider a Roll-Leather Collar [see Photo 2]. These are designed work with the long coat, moving freely round the dog's neck without tangling in the coat, nor damaging the coat caused by matting and rubbing that the flat collar in Photo 1 will cause.

There are many types of leads, I prefer normal leather or soft fabric lead and a long training line are essentials for your dog kit.

A word about extending or retractable leads.

Do not use extending or retractable leads. These are not suitable for dog walking. They are dangerous if the line makes contact with yours or your dog's skin. They can also be counter-productive to teaching a dog not to pull on a lead.

No harness for pups

Harnesses are good for adult working-dogs—Guide Dogs, Tracking Dogs, Assistance Dogs and Sled Dogs etc. While I know there are many new types of harnesses now claiming to encourage dogs not to pull, and to work with the owner, I am yet to be convinced. The harness is a great tool designed to give your dog the freedom to drive, pull and lead, these are certainly not the traits you want to be teaching your puppy.

For training your puppy I recommend a normal collar and lead. There are occasionally rare exceptions when I would recommend a harness for a dog.

Other essential items

ID tag: for the collar is a must have, whether she is micro chipped or not. In the UK the Control of Dogs order 1992 states, 'A dog must wear a collar with the owner's name, address (including post code) engraved or written on it or on an ID tag. Telephone number is optional, but is recommended.' You can be fined up to £500. For failing to comply with this order.

Shampoo: The correct shampoo is essential to prevent irritating your dog's skin. *For more details, see chapter 10, Handling and Grooming.*

Brush and comb: Do a little research on what tools are required for your chosen dog, it can vary considerably depending on the breed you have chosen *For more details, see chapter 10, Handling and Grooming.*

Dog bowls: - One for food and one for water – Your dog should have her own bowls, and not eat from yours. Stainless steel is best as it is easier to sterilise. Some dogs have been known to be allergic to the plastic ones and they are also quite keen to use them as chew toys. Also, holes in plastic provides a breeding ground for bacteria.

Dog crate: Select a crate of the correct size for your pup and its growth expectations. A crate should be just big enough for your dog to stand up, turn round and lie down. If you buy one to last into adulthood, you will need to put a partition in otherwise your puppy may use one end as a toilet area. Under no circumstances is this to be encouraged, even though some trainers may recommend placing puppy pads at one end of it, this is an extremely poor method to implement and can create a confused puppy as you are forcing them to go against the grain and toilet by their bed. *See chapter 6, Den Training.*

Food: Select the best quality you can, you will benefit from feeding quality food in the long run. A good breeder will be happy to guide you. You cannot and should not rely on the dog food packaging to guide you with what is in it. There are few laws governing what needs to be put on dog food packaging. Things aren't always what they seem. Do your research on the internet, it is all there for you to read, so that you are clear on what you are feeding.

If you decide to feed raw meat do your homework properly, pre-minced raw in pet shops can be equally as bad as some canned or some dry foods. Just because it says raw, doesn't make it good. It is important that you feed a quality balanced diet. You must know how to feed raw properly and what foods the dog needs to balance all her nutrients; you cannot guess at it as you go along. Personally I feed a good quality dry food but my dogs also have a variety of fresh food added to it on a daily basis. I believe, that variety creates a stronger stomach and less allergic reactions to foods.

Puppy supplies check list

- ✓ Dog bed/Crate/Play pen depending on what space you have and what method of training you want to do.
- ✓ Bedding – Vet fleece bedding is about the best there is.
- ✓ Dog bowls — 1 for water and 1 for food.
- ✓ Chew toys — make sure they are suitable for puppies, as listed above.
- ✓ Puppy collar and lead — make sure it's safe for your breed of dog.
- ✓ ID tag — your name and address, telephone number is optional, but recommended.
- ✓ Foods — check with breeder what you need to get and stick with it for at least a week or expect to have an upset stomach. Feed the best in quality you can.
- ✓ Toys & Chews — make sure the toys and chews are safe for puppy and that pieces can't come off them.

Today is collection day

If you are anything like me, this will be a very exciting day, sometimes common sense goes out the window, so it is a really good idea to plan ahead and make a list, have everything ready that you will need to help the day run smoothly, minimising stress for you and your pup.

I hope that by now you have done your homework and know what to expect from the breeder and what paperwork and information you should expect to receive from them.

If you are purchasing a pedigree/purebred dog, it is a good idea to check with your country's Kennel Club Website for details of what you should expect to receive. These days it is all on there, and there is no excuse for not knowing. Whilst there are many good breeders who will keep you well informed, there are those who will tell you what 'they' think you need to know and operate very much on a 'need to know basis', they will only tell you if you ask. There are also those who aren't necessarily hiding anything, they just don't think that people will understand the information or that they would be interested in it, so they don't volunteer it.

If you don't ask questions you only have yourself to blame and you must accept responsibility for not having done your homework. The UK Kennel Club website has a section called 'Find A Puppy', this is extremely informative and a good place to start to help you ask the right questions.

Your visit with the breeder

The breeder may have given you guidelines for collecting and transporting your puppy, but just in case, here are some helpful guidelines.

Make an appointment time with your breeder and stick to it. Remember you may not be the only person collecting a puppy and therefore being reliable with your arrangements are essential to avoid frustration for the breeder and to give you maximum time to gain all the info you need from the breeder.

Ideally collect your puppy in the morning, this allows her some time at home to acclimatise and adjust before settling down for the night.

Preferably take someone with you, who can take charge of the puppy on the journey home, (not a child). They can help take charge of the puppy, so that you are not distracted, they can help your puppy feel secure rather than placing her in a crate to roll around on her own. She is more likely to feel sick if placed in a crate and has to adjust to finding her balance on the journey, she may never have experienced a car before, other than to visit the vet for her first vaccine, unless the breeder has done car journeys and acclimatised her to the movement. Sickness would not be a good start for a first car journey and could have a lasting effect on how she travels in the future.

If, however you have no option but to make the trip alone, take a small pet carrier, i.e. a cat carrier (rather than placing your pup in a crate) and put plenty of good bedding in it so that she is well cushioned and cannot slide around. Your puppy will feel more secure, and you can have it strapped in on the front seat beside you or in the front foot-well where you can reassure and keep an eye on your puppy.

If you have children ideally, leave them at home. Do not take them with you to collect the puppy, in fact if your children are school age, it is better if they are at school when puppy arrives home, allowing your puppy some time to adjust without the noise and excitement that comes with being a child. It can be quite overwhelming for a puppy. Your visit with the breeder could take an hour or two, children can become fractious and noisy when bored and there is a lot of information the breeder will need to share with you. They may not be happy if you can't concentrate with children distracting you.

A travel bag with some essential items in case of emergency is a must, i.e. kitchen roll, wipes, a towel, clean bedding, pooh bags, water and a bowl. A collar and lead, just in case you need to stop and put her down somewhere, better to be safe than sorry. The list may seem extreme, but I guarantee you if you don't have it you will need it, better to be safe than sorry.

Check list for collecting your puppy

- ✓ Small pet carrier (cat carrier size, obviously depending on the size of your pup).
- ✓ A Towel or blanket. (x2 in case of an accident)
- ✓ Kitchen Towel for wipe ups.
- ✓ Scent free baby wipes, just in case your pup is sick.
- ✓ A puppy collar and lead, for emergency stops.
- ✓ Poo bags.
- ✓ Water and a bowl.

05 Arriving Home with your Pup – What to expect

In this chapter

- It's okay to be confused and scared
- Introducing your pup to your other dog
- When Mr Tibs met Twyla
- Introducing your pup to your cat safely

- Ways to help a cat and pup adapt to each other
- A cat amongst the dogs
- Introducing your pup to your children
- Guide dog puppy Kirby meets the children
- Shaping best friends – Dogs and children
- Summary for a happy child/happy dog

It's okay to be confused and scared

Confusion and a little scared is quite to be expected, (and that's just you). I jest not, it doesn't take long before most new owners at some point think, 'What have I done?' It's natural, but remember if it's confusing for you, imagine how your puppy is feeling.

Try to see things from your pup's point of view. Last night she was asleep, safe and secure, with her mother, brothers and sisters and then the next night she is in a strange place that she has never seen or even smelt before, in a bed where she is expected to sleep all on her own. Wouldn't you be frightened and stressed? Be patient, but start how you mean to go on. Following the crate-den training and night time training method, will help avoid over stressing your puppy and your family.

First impressions count

On arriving at your home, toilet your puppy outside in your chosen toilet spot, (hopefully you have already allocated this area) before taking her indoors, this first step matters. Once she has toileted, take her indoors and allow her to walk around the one room where she is going to be spending most of her time. This should be the room where her den is. As soon as she gets tired she must be placed in her den to sleep. Do not allow her to fall asleep where she chooses, unless it is in her bed. This is your first step at creating the right impression for your pup.

If you have another dog at home, the introductions need to begin, before taking your pup into the house, to avoid the possibility of any problems. If you don't have another dog, cat or children, skip the next sections and go straight to Den Training. Otherwise read the relevant section.

Introducing your pup to your older dog

If you already have another dog, then obviously they need to meet, so that they can adapt to each other's smells and get to know one another. However, careful handling of the introduction must be put in place so that both the puppy and the adult dog have a positive experience.

Ideally if your new dog was older (i.e. not a puppy) I would advise meeting on neutral territory, however with a new puppy this is not so easy for obvious health & safety reasons. Here are a few steps to help make the transition go smoother.

Do not bring your pup straight into the home when you arrive back with her, this can cause stress and tension from the outset and will not provide the harmony you are hoping for.

What I have found works as an alternative to meeting on neutral territory is, to put your puppy in a crate, outside in the garden or yard if possible. Do not hold your pup in your arms when introducing her, this can create tension. If you have more than one dog then allow the youngest of your dogs out to find the pup first, watch how the pup reacts and how your dog reacts to the pup.

After a few minutes of gauging your dog's reaction to the new addition, you can use happy tones to indicate to your dog that this is exciting and a good thing. I usually say something like, 'What have you found'? This makes the adult a little excited about their find and immediately from my tone they think this is a good thing. If you have multiple dogs, then repeat the process with each one separately.

I had one of my dogs when I brought my new puppy home, completely ignored her and the crate, as though he couldn't see them, he walked around with his tail wagging sniffing every area of the patio, other than where the crate was. He was telling me, 'I don't want to see her'. He knew she was there obviously, but just didn't want to acknowledge her. If the pup had been free and bounded up to a dog exhibiting this behaviour, the likelihood is that the pup would be snapped at. The crate offers your puppy protection from itself and whichever behaviour it may exhibit.

Some pups will appear wary when approached by the bigger dog, but others behave like a goofball with no concern or thought that anything bad will happen. They will bounce up to the adult and swing on them and put their paws on them, this can spell disaster if the adult feels the need to teach puppy a lesson. Putting paws on another dog that you have no relationship with is extremely disrespectful in a dog's mind and a dominant gesture, even though your puppy may not mean it that way, it will most likely be met with reprimand.

Within a relatively short period of time they will be best friends if the introductions are kept under your tight control. Once the adult dog is aware of the pup, take pup inside and put her in her pen where she can acclimatise safely to the environment. Do not let her down to run around with the adult, this is premature, even if you think the other dog is fine.

Remember, up to now this turf has belonged to your adult dog and any dog coming in and milling around, touching what doesn't belong to her, may be seen as a threat, 'even if it is a pup'. Contrary to the old myth that an adult dog would never hurt a pup, this is not always true. She may not intend to hurt her, but it doesn't take much due to the size difference, and the adult may not use discretion when teaching the pup her manners.

Outside in the garden is the best place to allow your new pup and adult to have their first few free interactions. It is more neutral and less confined than indoors. Your adult can outwit the pup easier and make a hasty retreat if he desires. You will be able to assess more accurately how your adult feels about the puppy.

After a few sessions outdoors, you will find they run into the house together and probably never look back. It will be as though they have always been together. However, you must still keep your pup in her separate area of the house, do not be tempted to leave the pup free to sleep with the adult. It can cause discord and create problems further down the road, no matter how cute it looks to you. It is not usually what the adult dog wants, even if they appear unbothered by it.

Be careful too, of the overzealous adult dog who is excited about this new arrival and playmate. He won't know how much rough and tumble a puppy can take and may knock her about too much. This can cause damage both mentally and physically. For these reasons I recommend introducing play sessions over the course of a few weeks. As your pup grows and becomes more stable on her feet.

When Mr Tibs met Twyla

Not all dogs welcome the newcomer with 'open paws', some can be quite put out that there is a newcomer in their home, no matter how young they are.

I remember my first Tibetan Terrier Mr Tibs, who absolutely loved pups. When Mr Tibs met a puppy in the street or on a walk, he could not contain his excitement, he would dance on his hind legs, rush up to them with tail wagging franticly and play bow to them, he simply loved pups, until that is, I brought home Twyla.

Mr Tibs was not an only dog, I already had a German Shepherd (Kassi) and a Labrador (Bracken), but I couldn't wait to bring him his own puppy home (well she was mine really, but I was happy to share).

The day of arrival came and our second Tibetan Terrier arrived (Twyla). They met outside on the patio, Mr Tibs took one quick sniff of her, and backed away rather quickly as though she had the plague, I was gutted. I could not believe it, he was having none of it and I found it quite difficult to understand at first, I found myself saying to him, 'But you love puppies!', as though that mattered to him. He did not want this puppy in his home, or did he? He simply ignored her, it was like she just didn't exist. If you called him into a room he would peer in the door and if she was there he would turn tail and go to another room.

When this happens, it can be quite upsetting, but don't let it be, try to keep your emotions in check, it will be short lived for most. What your dog is doing when this happens, is establishing himself with the newcomer. He is doing what we all should probably do, (but of course we don't) playing it cool to establish some ground rules, once these are established he will let the pup enter his world, on his terms and a wonderful relationship can blossom.

I remember Mr Tibs clearly telling Twyla where she stood, every time I offered them a treat together, he would show his teeth at her, and I would remind him with a strong 'Hey!' that I was still in charge, but every time she took a treat from me, even from across the room he would curl his lip, just to make sure she understood that he was not impressed and did not approve of her sharing. Now I find it very amusing thinking about it, but at the time I was horrified and quite upset, but I needn't have been.

She was very respectful of his signals toward her and I never ever allowed her to invade his space through this period of adjustment, she was never allowed to bound up to him while he was in this period of establishing the ground rules.

We only had Twyla approximately two weeks when the first snow arrived, I took both dogs out into the garden to enjoy the moment. Twyla was uncertain of the white stuff and just sat looking around. Mr Tibs was very familiar with it and was very excited.

I was fortunate to have my camera to record the first ever play-bow that Tibs made to Twyla. The photograph opposite brings back so many beautiful memories of the fun these two dogs brought me. This was the start of a beautiful relationship. There was never a cross growl or a quarrel between them, and she adored him as her friend and respected him as her mentor, as we all did. Mr Tibs was my first Tibetan Terrier and taught me so much about what makes this wonderful breed tick.

Mr Tibs' first play-bow

The moral of this story is, do not try to force the friendship, if you have a dog that is not happy or interested in the new arrival, relax into it and follow these simple guidelines.

- Allow him or her to control their own situation and they need to always have space to get away from the puppy.
- Don't allow your puppy to bounce up to them, over them or around them.
- Don't allow your puppy to share his bed, or take his toys. (No matter how cute it looks)
- Don't allow your puppy to eat from his bowl.
- Don't force your adult dog to be in the same room as the pup, if they don't want to be.

Keep your emotions in check, don't feel sorry for your other dog because he looks unhappy, his behaviour will be for the pup's benefit. Allow him to come and go as he pleases. If he does enter the room where the pup is, control the pups behaviour not his, and it will all work out in the end.

If he sees you controlling the pup, he will know where the pup fits into the team. If you allow the pup to do what she wants and go where she wants because she is a 'puppy', he will lose respect for you and the puppy. He may not show his disapproval now, but he is more likely to, as the pup grows and becomes more challenging. He will feel the need to put the pup in her place as he may see you as having let her go unchecked, remember someone has to be leader.

Introducing your pup to your cat safely

Dogs and cats can live really well together, some of them even become extremely good play mates. The litters that I have bred have all had the good fortune of learning what a cat is and that you don't get to chase the cat.

To introduce your pup and cat to each other, is somewhat different than introducing another dog. Much of this meeting needs to go at your cats pace, your cat needs to control how this goes and the pace it goes at. You cannot force a friendship between them. However, there are a few things you can do to help the process along.

The most important point to remember is, your pup needs to be kept secure in his pen or crate, when your cat is about. He must not be given the opportunity run up to the cat, two results are possible if this happens:

1) Your cat stands his ground and the pup gets a beating, which could be quite serious if the cat catches her eye.

2) Your cat may run, which means your pup now learns that if you run at something, it runs from you and the chase is on. This then allows her to develop her chase and prey drive instincts, which will likely be a problem later on, for your cat and other animals she may encounter.

Ways to help a cat and pup adapt to each other

1. Take a small soft blanket, which has her scent on it, from your pup's crate and put it where your cat can sniff it and lie on it if he wants to.

2. Then after a few days put the blanket back in with the pup, so that she can smell the cat on it. This allows them to become accustomed to the scent of each other from a distance. You can do this blanket exchange a few times over the course of a week. You will see your cat become more curious but more relaxed each time he smells it.

3. Your cat should be allowed and encouraged to move around the home as normal, while the pup remains in a confined area where she can see the cat coming and going, but can't go after him.
4. Your pup only gets freedom in her room, when the cat is not present. It is very important that your cat knows that the pup can't and won't get to him. You will find, that your cat's confidence and curiosity will get the better of him and he will move closer and closer to the pup. The old saying 'Curiosity killed the cat', is for good reason, they are nosy and can't resist investigating.

Allowing your puppy to run up to the cat repeatedly, seldom ends well and very seldom stops in my experience. Most pups will always want to chase the cat if allowed to do this, as its good fun amusing themselves at the cat's expense and practicing their chase skills

Dandy and Amara

Give your cat the opportunity to explore your pup's crate-den, when she is out to toilet or in another room. You will find at some point he goes nose to nose with the pup through the bars of her puppy pen or crate. He may begin rubbing his body on the crate and thumbing his nose in the air at the pup in a superior way.

Time is key and you need to be patient and not try to force the two together. Let it happen naturally from a distance. Distance breeds respect. The same applies when raising children with a puppy.

Remember dogs are a creature of habit, if they never get to chase the cat, the chances are they never will. It is your responsibility to see that this doesn't happen.

A cat amongst dogs
Often a beautiful relationship of trust develops between animals of the opposite species, this was the case for my dog Mr Tibs and his best friend and playmate, Dandy the cat. The following is a small glimpse of how beautiful a relationship can be between a dog and a cat.

Dandy and Mr Tibs were very trusting of each other, they would play-fight as though they were two dogs playing, but it appeared they created their own set of rules for the game. Once Dandy left the floor and jumped to a surface, he was out of bounds and couldn't be touched, even though Tibs could have reached him. However, if his feet left the surface to jump to another surface then the game was on and Tibs could take him out of the air, which he did on numerous occasions.

Tibs would show his Tibetan patience by sitting calmly alongside the surface that Dandy was sitting on, and he would sit, and sit, and sit some more, until Dandy made his move and Bam! He would have him straight to the floor. Interestingly they only played these games when I was present, a lot of the time they were found curled up asleep together. I am certain the games were as much for my enjoyment as theirs. I regret that I never videoed their antics. What always surprised me was that neither ever got hurt. Tibs never received a scratch from Dandy and Dandy never got hurt by Tibs, despite how rough the game could appear. If Tibs was getting a bit rough, Dandy would make a particular sound and Tibs would stop instantly.

Sadly, Mr Tibs is no longer with me but Dandy is still very much part of the dog den at almost 20 years old. The previous photo shows Dandy today with my youngest TT who loves to groom him. Although his rough and tumble days are far behind him, he still loves the dogs to clean him and asks regularly for the pups to do so. Two over-exuberant 16 month-old Tibetan Terriers, wash him vigorously at any given the opportunity, but only under my careful supervision.

Introducing your pup to your children

As I said earlier, collecting your pup on a school day is a great idea. Children get very excited at the thought of the arrival of a new puppy, and rightly so. Therefore, collecting your pup and arriving home without the shrieks of children around is the best option. This also allows your pup the chance to take in the sights and smells of the new home without added noise and a whole lot of fuss

At the risk of sounding a kill-joy, your pup is not a toy for the children, she is not something to be passed around and fought over. I have seen perfectly good pups turn into frustrated, bad tempered pups within two to three weeks, due to over-handling and being grabbed at by children. Both child and pup need to be protected from each other. Unpleasant experiences of the child may store in the mind of a puppy, as someone not to be trusted. This is not a good footing to get off on.

Your pup will also learn quickly to treat the child as one of its litter mates if they are allowed to roll around the floor with her. Unfortunately, for the child your pup is going to win, they are not compatible rough and tumble play mates, but they can learn to play the right games together.

Guide dog puppy Kirby meets the children
Sometimes despite all the planning, things just don't happen the way you expect them too.

Many years ago when my children were little I decided I would like to become a Puppy Walker for the 'Guide Dogs for the Blind Association'. I had one child who was six, and at school and another who was nursery age. I was already a dog trainer and shared my home with a very well trained, White German shepherd called (Kassi). I decided it was time to add to our home and rather than buy our own puppy, I wanted to give something back using the experience I had, I chose the Guide Dogs for the Blind Association as my charity to become involved with.

Having passed my assessment with the Guide Dogs, the arrival date for our first puppy was fast approaching. I am not sure how it works now, but at the time, they gave the prospective puppy walker a video to watch ahead of time. The video was of a puppy walker receiving their new puppy, in the video the Guide Dog assessor arrived with a small pet carrier and out came this small cute, perfectly formed little

Labrador puppy, quiet, subdued and looking bewildered after a long car journey. It was all very lovely and quite perfect.

As my big day arrived for our first puppy to grace our home, I had prepared my children as much as one can, that they must be quiet and not touch the pup unless I told them they could in the beginning. I explained that the pup would be frightened and would need time to adjust. It was arranged that the children would not be home when the pup arrived, so that I could deal with the details and help him to settle.

The hour arrived and the Guide Dog van drew up, at the front of the house, I was so excited. I waited by our front door, there was a lot of fumbling and noise in the back of the van, Helen (the advisor) popped her head up and said, 'You did say you would have anything, right'? I laughed nervously, wondering what on earth was coming.

Suddenly, a huge puppy appeared. Who, I might add, looked more like Scooby Doo than the *Andrex* puppy. He tumbled out of Helen's arms and into my garden, (no small pet carrier keeping him secure). He then galloped towards me and straight past me, through the front door, skidding on the wooden floor, turned the corner and straight into the living room, diving head first into the children's toy box. I looked on in disbelief.

The only thing I remember saying is 'Where's the puppy in the video?' To which she replied, 'We ran out of them, this one had your name marked all over it. He's trouble', she exclaimed, 'and will need a firm hand'.

Apparently the journey had not been a quiet one as he had shredded every last piece of newspaper in the van and roughed and tumbled creating a commotion on the whole journey unsettling the other pups.

Sometime later the children arrived home. Within minutes my youngest, Nathan, was hiding up on the back of the couch whilst Kirby (the puppy) was swinging on my daughter Jamie's braids. Who by the way, was trying hard not to touch him as per mum's instructions, bless her. I quickly had to amend those instructions, to prevent the mauling and ragging that was about to happen.

So the moral of this story is, if you get this unlucky (or lucky, depending upon you how you look at it) and have a full-on tornado land in your home then sometimes you have to adapt your best laid plans.

In case you are wondering, Kirby became an amazing guide dog who did grow very, very tall, he was a Lab X Retriever and went on to work with an owner who was six-foot-five-inches tall.

Shaping best friends — dogs and children

Children and dogs can be wonderful together, but they can also be a recipe for disaster. Space creates respect, let me explain further.

Children and pups, both are young and learning about the world. Both can be trying and testing at times. Put them together and leave them to get on with it and one will soon get fed up with the other and get angry and frustrated and somebody will get hurt.

Children are experimental, that is how they learn. Do not leave them with your pup where they may try things out on them—it could be disastrous.

 No matter how well behaved you think your child is, or how well you think you have raised them, this is not about being mean or naughty, they are simply doing what they do best, being a child. Do not assume they will be good around a pup. They will do the unexpected and they may hurt your puppy and break her trust in them.

Dogs are pretty much of the same behaviour as a child, they test everything and try everything out. They will try biting, ragging and humping the children, if the child is unable to deal with it, then the pup begins to feel that they are more powerful and assertive than the child. This his can create problems in their development together.

Summary for a happy child and a happy dog.

Dog Training schools that encourage your children to be involved are a great idea, the more you encourage your children to do the right things with the puppy the better the relationship will be.

It is an extremely good rule to implement from the beginning that your children are not allowed to pick puppy up. No matter what size the pup is going to be. Too many pups are injured from being dropped by children picking them up. Children do not pick pups up correctly and this can be extremely uncomfortable for the pup. Most children lift the pup under the tummy which causes a lot of pressure on the pup's internal organs and is very uncomfortable. Your puppy will soon dislike the child approaching if this is allowed to happen and may very quickly become snappy when approached from behind because she assumes she is going to be lifted.

Most pups on entering their new home gravitate towards the young in the home, as they identify with them. They are fun, excitable, high-pitched and always busy. All the things that attract a puppy! However, how your pup plays and how a child plays are two very different things. Pups only know how to play as a dog, using their mouths, and their paws. They learn textures and tastes by mouthing and they learn to control by biting.

Children play human games, with their hands and toys as tools. Pups rough and tumble, biting on one another and learning who is the strongest and how to win the game. This is not generally the same game children play on a daily basis, nor should children and pups be encouraged to play rough and tumble together. The two are not compatible as play mates to just throw together. Your child will not be able to endure the pressure from the pup's needle-sharp teeth.

It is not a good model to allow puppy to practice this as she will quickly learn that she has the upper hand when it comes to who rules the floor. She will take and chew your child's toys and very quickly everything your child has becomes fair game.

Children and pups must learn how to play and how to interact in a suitable manner over time together. Your puppy needs to learn to play human games and play by your rules. They must learn how to interact amicably, but both have to learn this and you must teach them both how to achieve this if harmony and respect are to develop between them. Learning to play the right games will make your child and your pup lifelong friends, and there is nothing greater.

06 Den Training your Pup

Den training is establishing the space that you want your puppy to occupy so that she knows the rules and boundaries, what is acceptable and what is not.

Den training prevents her from getting into trouble. It is also a great aid for helping with toilet training.

Den training is essential to creating a balanced family dog. Your dog's den could be a crate, a pen or it may even be a small room with a normal dog bed in it.

For me, one of the best concepts in dog training was the creation of Crate training. This provides our dogs with a secure place, somewhere they can rest undisturbed. When they are in their den, they feel secure. For us, the den keeps our furry friend out of trouble when we aren't there to supervise, which in turn keeps them safe. It's pretty much like putting a baby in a play pen. Crate-Den training is the fastest method of toilet training there is, if taught correctly it avoids all toilet accidents from happening.

Like it or loathe it

Some people like it and some loathe it. The latter of the two believes crate training to be cruel, unnatural and unnecessary, but for me this is a not a rational way of thinking. Taking a puppy away from is mum and brothers and sisters, isn't particularly normal, but we do it. Dogs are domesticated and as I have already said, they are adaptable. They are more comfortable when they know where they are meant to be and are often left developing insecurities when they are left to make their own choices, roaming around the house with no one to guide them. The crate provides continuity for how they are going to live and provides a security. They know where they belong and where they fit in when provided with a secure area.

I want to talk about what is natural for a moment. Digging a hole in the ground as a den to sleep in or give birth in is natural, or crawling under something to hide and rest is natural, this enables three sides of the dog to be protected at any one time, but this is not practical for our delightful house dog, so we are offering her a chance to have a little of the security that is 'natural', by offering her a homemade den, the only difference is a door. I have never known a dog who was introduced to the crate correctly who didn't love their home made den.

The den is going to be where your puppy lives until all the house rules have been established. This will be your puppy's den until she reaches maturity, which may take as long as 18 months to 2 years. Some breeds, like many of the gundogs and working breeds, may take longer to mature, restrictions  may need to be in place until they are 3 or 4 years old, depending on the individual. Patience is essential if you are to avoid unwanted problems from developing. Both you and your dog will benefit enormously from this in the long run, if used correctly.

As mentioned earlier, if you are not in favour of using a crate for den training, you must still come up with a location within your home, the kitchen, utility room or the down stairs loo, where your dog can be restricted. Please note, that my suggested locations are mostly places found to the rear of many properties. Ideally your dog's den should be located away from your main entrance and exit. Not being able to see you leave the house, or see people entering, is also very beneficial to preventing other problems from developing later on. Placing the den as close to the door as possible, that the puppy will exit through to toilet, will also aid you in your training.

The crate should be big enough for your dog as an adult to stand up, turn round and lie down. The less room she has to wander around, the less pacing she will do and the less likely she is to need to toilet and the better she will settle. Movement stimulates the bladder and bowel movements. If you buy an adult size crate, then you will need to put in a temporary divider to make the crate smaller while she is a puppy. Otherwise, she may choose to use one end as her toilet area and this should never be encouraged. Do not put newspaper or puppy pads in the crate, as this will encourage her to toilet in it and this should never be encouraged.

The benefits of providing a crate-den

✓ It is more likely to prevent territorial issues from developing.
✓ Your dog will learn to switch off and sleep when you're out shopping or at work, making him a more contented friend.
✓ The den will be your dog's bed. Dogs do not like to soil their beds which means they will cry when they need to go out, you must respond every time.
✓ It's a place which prevents bad habits from developing. For example, your dog isn't going to chew your table leg or climb on the work surfaces when you're not around if she's secure in her den. If you have a dog who has previously had a bad experience with crate training, and you would rather not revisit crate training then please look for an alternative location, as suggested above. For this pre-vaccination training to work, you must choose a place that is small and where your dog can be contained from the rest of the house.

Why your pup should not sleep in your bed

No matter how much you like the idea, your dog should not share your bed and it is a bad plan, at least in the early days. However, (don't close the book yet) over time this may not be a problem, if you have a real desire to have your dog in your bed. Providing that the rules and boundaries are established first and your puppy has learnt to accept sleeping where 'you' chose then later she may be invited to join you on the bed, but not before she is at least two years old.

In your bedroom, your scent is at its strongest and this area should be kept for you as the leader and head of the house. Your dog should not be encouraged to add her scent to yours in the early stages of developing your relationship together. Some dogs will take to weeing on their owner's bed due to the desire to cover your scent. This is never good. Establishing the rules and boundaries at the beginning will stop things from ever reaching this stage.

Ideally your dog should sleep as far away from your bedroom as possible, for example in the kitchen or utility room. If you really need to have your puppy sleep in the same room as you, then it is even more important that you use a crate as her den to control where she goes through the night and prevent her from attempting to get on the bed.

The den training, I am going to take you through is using a crate, this is my preferred method of training for a puppy. This section is fairly comprehensive and if you are unsure about the benefits of crate-den training, hopefully this will help you view it differently.

It will not matter where she begins sleeping in the crate-den, as she will transfer easily to wherever you move her crate. The crate-den becomes home, her safe-haven and the place she looks forward to switching off in. *For further information, see chapter 9, Night-Time Toilet Training.*

Remember, this is not going to last forever (unless you want it to of course). This restriction on your dog, is to help her fit with your family and provide you with the dog you want long-term. You are shaping your dog to fit with your situation and creating the best companion for you and your family, while at the same time creating a contented dog by preventing your puppy from making mistakes and subsequently being told off.

Den training leads to faster toilet training and prevents undesirable behaviours from developing, such as separation anxiety. It keeps your puppy out of trouble, making you happier, creating a more relaxed pup, allowing for better bonding and a more enjoyable time for all.

Quite often a puppy will choose to make its bed under a table or behind the settee, the den you choose to give her, offers a better alternative than this, particularly if you drape a cover over the top. The den you provide is your chosen area for your dog rather than your dog choosing the area, which can create possessive tendencies if allowed to develop.

Choosing the right crate for a den

There are many, many makes and types of crates available on the market, the one you choose is down to preference and which suits your situation.

Sky Kennel: Made from fibreglass and closed-in except for a wire door on the front, with slots on the side. Lots of people don't like these because the dog can't see all around. Personally I have used all three types mentioned here and although I use the wire crate, I find my  pups preferred the closed-in type and seemed to feel more secure. However, for a very timid dog the open variety may prove to be the better alternative. This type of crate also holds more heat for puppies, although be careful when leaving your dog on a warm day, best to leave the door open, as they can tend to get a bit warm inside.

I use one of these for traveling in the car, as they are very safe, they are designed for traveling on aircraft, hence the name.

Fold Flat Indoor Kennels: Made from Metal, the dog can see all around rather like a cage and by far the most popular type of crate. The crate folds flat for transporting or  for storage. The bottom is fitted with a removable plastic tray or metal tray for easy cleaning. Place a suitable blanket or bedding in it.

With young puppies, a box or comfy bed placed inside the den is best for comfort and heat. My experience with the metal den is, my dogs generally only need a light blanket as they often like to move it away and lie on the tray if they get too warm, so don't over fill the den with bedding.

The Home-made Kennel: There are various alternatives for this. The converted cupboard. The first indoor kennel I ever used was a broom cupboard in the kitchen, which had the door removed and fitted with baby gate covered in suitable wire. It was cheap and could be reused at a later date.

A square wooden unit cut to size, the inside covered with rubber to prevent damp getting through either way and a detachable metal door fixed to the front. (Incidentally this was the all time favourite with the puppies and the one I had most trouble weaning the puppies out off). With a bit of imagination, you will be amazed at what you can come up with.

Pop-up Kennels: Made with fabric and netting, very similar to a pop up tent and becoming very popular. These are not to be recommended for housing your dog at home, while you are out. They are easily destroyed and the dog can very quickly chew her way out. However, they  are ideal for taking on holiday with you while in a hotel room where you are permanently with your well-trained dog.

Den training – where to start

So, you have made a choice and purchased your puppy's crate-den. Let's get started on understanding how this works and teaching your puppy to enjoy the den. The den must be introduced from the minute your puppy enters your home, if you want to avoid crying protests and a stressed puppy.

How does this work?

Your puppy has her area where she is allowed to eat, sleep and play when you can't watch her. **Sleep** is the key word here. This is where people often make the biggest mistake.

Your puppy should sleep only in her den area, nowhere else in the house, not by your feet, under the table, on your lap etc. The crate-den, is her sleeping area. This provides continuity and leaves your dog in no doubt as to who the house belongs to, as well as where she fits in. By teaching your dog to enjoy her own space and relax in her own company and routinely go to sleep in her den, you create the habit for her—dogs are 'naturally', creatures of habit.

Scenario: Your pup is running around playing, and then she grows tired and wanders off to find a spot to sleep. This becomes the normal pattern very quickly. Wherever your puppy sleeps, becomes hers (in her mind). It also becomes her right to choose where she sleeps. In a relatively short space of time, you will find she starts to object to being asked to go into her crate or den area, because you have allowed her to choose where she sleeps.

At the risk of boring you, 'dogs are a creature of habit', if the only place they are allowed to sleep is their den, they will never object to it, they will love it and look forward to switch-off time. Every time she needs to sleep, show her to the den, once she settles in it, close the door.

It is part of her natural instinct to keep the den area clean, but also to prevent predators being attracted to the den area. Your puppy being restricted in a den, cannot wake up and wander freely without alerting you. She will ask you to let her out by crying, as she will not want to soil where she sleeps.

If your puppy has joined your home and you already have a resident dog, it is even more important to follow a set structure. Your pup must sleep where you put her and not be allowed to sleep with the other dog, no matter how cute it may seem and no matter how accepting your other dog may seem to be towards the pup. Your pup should not get a choice, otherwise you may have a pup that not only can't be without your company, but also walks in the shadow of your other dog and cannot function well as an individual.

Introducing your pup to the den

I recommend den training to most owners I meet. Den training is suitable for both puppies and for the older dog too. The first reaction I get from people is sometimes one of shock. Some are even horrified at the thought of putting their dog into what seems like a 'cage'. It may take a little time, to recognise it, but once people have stopped thinking of the crate as a cage and more as a den and safe-haven, most agree to try it out.

Without exception, I have never had anyone regret using the den. Most usually say they can't imagine how they would have lived without one. The mistakes some people make are usually:

- Taking the den away from the dog too soon in her development (i.e. before she has fully matured) sometimes means she relapses into unwanted behaviours such as chewing and toileting indoors and using the den inappropriately.
- Leaving your pup cooped-up for too long and for too frequent periods. This can lead to a very frustrated dog causing excessive barking, compulsive licking and biting of their selves.

Please don't dismiss this very successful system of training until you understand all the benefits of what 'den training' is, and please follow the instructions carefully and thoroughly. Crate-den training is beneficial for you, but equally beneficial for your dog, but it won't be if she is spending hours on end in it.

The following method of den training has proven to be completely successful in my thirty-years as a dog trainer.

Helping your puppy adapt

Please remember these important points

✓ The den must always be associated with something good.
✓ Take the introductions slowly.

60

✓ The den must never be used for punishment.

✓ The den must never be used because you haven't got time to play, train or work with your dog.

Settling your puppy into a crate-den

Make sure that your den is set up before puppy arrives. It is probably best to set the den in the kitchen where you can keep puppy company and keep an eye on her to begin with. If you put her in a room and leave her she will become stressed, which will create stress for all of you.

You will also need a crate by your bed, in the bedroom. It is ok to make do with the one crate and just moved it to your bedroom at night, but if you want to have two, that's find too. The crate in your bedroom is only temporary to help puppy settle (she will not be remaining in your bedroom) and to ensure you and your family don't have disturbed sleep trust me this is the best method and you will not regret it.

o   Place a comfortable blanket or large towel in the den.

Secure the door of the den open, so that it doesn't move which could scare your puppy, while they are moving around and getting use to it. Many dogs learn to dislike the crate because of a bad introduction like being caught by the door when a puppy, prevention is always better than cure.

Allow your puppy to explore the room while you are with her, and encourage her to interact with you and toys. Play with her by the den. If at first your dog appears scared or wary of the den when she approaches it, begin by feeding a tasty treat near to it or if she will play with a toy, have a game with her as this will take her mind of it. Most puppies take to the crate-den very quickly. At 8 weeks old, it won't take long for her to tire, as she will have had a busy day. As soon as she starts to tire, encourage her with a treat or toy to the den, if she is reluctant pick her up and put her into the den.

At this stage, don't close the door, just sit by the den and wait. If she gets up and leaves the den (and she most likely will), just wait until she finds a spot to lie down on the floor, as soon as she does pick her up and put her back in the den. Keep repeating this until she is suddenly too tired to move out of the den. By lifting her when she lies down you are communicating to her that you don't want her to lie where she has chosen. When she settles in the den, close the door of the den and leave her to sleep.

○ When she wakes she will need the toilet instantly, so be on hand to take her out straight away.

A chew, suitable for puppies to gnaw on, is also a good idea, often they want to lie in a secure area to eat it. The den is the ideal place for this. A toy that can be stuffed with treats such as a Kong, is a good option for helping to take her mind of things, it will also tire her out and help to settle quicker in her den.

Have some small morsels of food and throw them into the den encouraging your puppy to go in and out of the den, until she is completely happy with entering the den. A puppy's reflexes are very slow in the early stages, so go slowly until she learns the throw movement. You may have to use meat as a definite appetiser, rather than a dog treat, to encourage her to go in, the smell from meat will help her locate it easier.

Feeding in the den

Feeding some of your pup's meals in the den is a good way of communicating another positive association with it.

Show your pup the bowl of food and lead her to the den with it, place the bowl far enough into the den that she has to enter to eat. As she enters the den introduce a cue word like 'den', 'bed' or 'place'. Say the cue each time she enters.

Your puppy will be on 3 to 4 meals a day, feed at least 1 or 2 of them inside the den and the other two feed by hand, this will encourage your puppy to bond with you and look to you for what she needs, by encouraging her to work for the food.

When placing the food in the den and she starts to eat, gently close the door and let her finish eating. Once finished, open the door and let her out. Do not move away or leave her while she is eating, your presence should always be apparent when your pup is eating her food.

If, when you put the meal in the den she refuses to enter, bring the meal nearer to the entrance and allow her to get used to the idea and to eat with just her head in the den, if she is wary. Keep your hand on the bowl, to give her confidence.

I don't find puppies usually have a problem with eating in the den, as they generally have no suspicion of it. It is usually more of a problem with the adult dog who has some experience of being closed in or, they have a fear of the unfamiliar.

If you are able to, close the door while she eats, open it straight away when she has finished and allow her to come out and take her to the toilet.

07 The Importance of a Good Feeding Regime

In this Chapter

- What you should know
- A guide to feeding your puppy
- The importance of wetting puppy meal
- Greedy feeders
- Fussy feeders
- Aggressive feeders
- Puppy table manners
- Preventing your puppy from becoming aggressive over food
- Should dogs graze?
- How much food should you feed your puppy?

What you should know

Many training methods have recorded that you should eat before your dog, indeed this is a method that for many years I subscribed to. You may have read, 'the pack leader always eats first'. This is not strictly true, while the pack leader may move in on the best part and choose their spot, often they will all eat at the same time. They must all keep their strength up in order to remain a strong team. It is no good if only the leader is well fed. However keeping order and calmness when food is due, is a beneficial exercise that will stand you in good stead as this communicates to your dog that you are in control of the food source and she should look to you for her supplies, not fight you for it.

A puppy should be fed 3 or 4 meals a day, when they first arrive in your home; this gives you and your family, plenty of opportunity to work with your dog creating good feeding habits. How the food is presented to your dog is an important exercise. There are a few steps you can take to ensure this happens correctly. It is important to take time at meal times and not rush the event, no matter how busy you are, feeding your pup properly should be a priority.

When preparing the food your puppy should be taught to give you space. Until she understands what is expected, either enlist the help

64

of a member of your family to keep control of her, or place her in her pen or crate so that she isn't jumping around you, demanding to be fed. In the early days of this, she may protest and complain about the restriction because she is hungry. Ignore the protest and carry on preparing her meal.

When feeding puppy, it is a good idea to hold the bowl on the floor, for at least one of the meals, or just rest your hand on it, (this is a good exercise for the children to get involved with). This will help her associate the food coming from you and keeping her free from the worry that you may take the food away.

If your pup walks away from her food, take it away. Do not allow her to pick and choose when to eat. If your pup was part of a pack of dogs and she moved away from her food another dog would swoop in and eat it in a second. This is the best lesson you can give your dog to convey that, you are a leader and in charge of the food source. 'See it, eat it or lose it', that's how your dog should view food, to maintain a healthy attitude to feeding.

Ace's Top Tip

Never practice the old art of taking your puppy's food away, when she is eating, even if your intention is to give it back. This can serve to make us protective and wary of people approaching our food. This can produce quite a severe reaction creating food guarding, depending upon a dog's nature. It is not a method I would ever recommend, although it is an age old practice.

A guide to feeding your puppy

I am not going to begin to tell you what type of food you should feed your puppy, that is a whole other book to write, if I were a dietician, which I'm not but I will give you a guide as to 'how' to feed your puppy, following the system I have used successfully for many years with various breeds.

In the early days, try to stick to what the breeder has advised you, for at least the first week, until your puppy has settled and adjusted to her new life, even if she does not seem to want it, don't start changing her food.

Lack of challenge = lack of appetite

Many puppies with in the first few days of arriving in their new home, go off their food, this could be due to stress, but is also quite likely that she just isn't very hungry now that food is on tap for her and she no longer has to compete with her litter mates for it.

The biggest mistake people make at this stage is to change the diet too soon. A change in diet at this stage in the settling process causes puppy to have an upset stomach, which then sets up a cycle of events. The owner then feels the need to find another food and now we have a puppy that is confused over what to eat and now has additional toilet issues to deal with.

Stick with what she has been use to and don't panic if she stops eating. Make the meals smaller and offer them at the normal time, she will begin eating again if you don't pander to her, and confuse her.

As I said earlier, dogs are designed to see it, eat it or lose it. If you practice this model she will consume her food when it is given to her. If she wanders away, during eating, give her a couple of moments, just in case she is trying to digest too big a mouthful, (it happens), if she comes back to it fine, if not remove it straight way. Do not offer her anything until the next meal time is due, she will not starve. If she were hungry she would have finished it.

She will quickly get the message. The worst feeding model is to leave a bowl of dry food down so that the dog can eat when she wants to. I know there are one or two dog foods on the market that encourage this, 'It Is Wrong'! Dogs are not grazers. This method of feeding causes so many problems that are easily avoided.

Fussy eaters – it's very boring seeing the same food sitting in a bowl all day.

Obesity – You cannot tell how much food a dog is having, If you just keep the bowl full all day, to name but two problems with this feeding regime.

I feed a variety of food to my dogs. I have followed the same model of feeding ever since I have owned dogs. I have never had a dog with a digestive problem, maybe I have been lucky, but I don't think so. I feed a quality complete food, (do your research), there is lots out there to help you. Ask what others feed their dogs, they will be only too willing to help. I introduce gradually something different to my dog's base meal, to get the stomach accustomed to different textures and tastes.

My dogs seldom have the same ingredient added to their base meal two nights running, which makes dinner time very exciting. Their base diet remains the same, but I add a small quantity of whatever I have cooked to it, this is usually what I have cooked the night before, I usually cook some extra and store in the fridge for the following day. The quantity added is usually no more than a two or three table spoons, depending on the dog, it is just to give flavour and encourage familiarity with other foods. For me, this makes a pup's tummy much stronger than if he only ever experiences dog food.

Whatever breed I have owned they have all had fairly cast iron stomachs. The only food I am cautious of feeding as it causes problems for all of my dogs is cooked turkey and cooked chicken.

The importance of wetting puppy meal

If you are feeding dry food to your puppy, make sure you wet it with a little boiled water, and allow it to soften, swell and cool, before feeding. When you feed dry without wetting it, many puppies will tire of eating it because of the effort of standing crunching it, particularly when they go through the same boring process 3 or 4 times a day and their gums are proving tender with new teeth pushing through.

Also a very important factor to me, dry food when it is wet swells, if you feed it to your puppy without wetting it, when it hits puppies stomach it will start to swell inside, this can cause discomfort for a puppy and digestive problems i.e. gas and wind. Make sure the food has done it's swelling before feeding to your puppy, you will also get a more accurate picture of how much food you pup is actually getting when you see it swollen with water, as some foods will double in size.

Contrary to popular belief they don't need to learn to chew on biscuits at dinner time for their teeth. In fact, it is very debatable as to whether biscuit will do anything for dental hygiene. For me the only real food that cleans a dog's teeth, is stripping meat of a bone. So if you don't feed bones, then you need to keep a check on the teeth as your dog gets two around 2 years+.

There are other ways that may help tackle the matter, by give puppy relevant chews, bones and toys to gnaw on you can also by oral paste for the teeth and oral liquid to put in the water, to help teeth from forming plaque, some of these work better than others, it is worth asking for opinions on these products. Allow your dog to enjoy her dinner by making it exciting and easy to eat, it should not be a chore.

Greedy feeders

These puppies eat like they might never see another meal. Until recently I would have said that my breed the Tibetan Terrier were seldom greedy feeders, until my two recent puppies that is, who eat exactly like this. However, I put this behaviour down to having never lost the competition of each other and the pack around them. If you have a greedy feeder, the easiest way to deal with this is to spread their food out so that they can't pick up huge volume in one swoop. You can either spread their food on the floor, although it's a bit messy or use a lap tray, having to move around to pick the food up, will slow the process down and your dog will gradually over time learn to control how she eats and that she doesn't need to eat at speed.

I know there are lots of new eating bowls designed to deal with this behaviour, personally I think my dogs would be incredibly frustrated and I think dinners times would be less pleasurable if they had to eat from some of these bowls, than simply spreading the food out. It's a lot cheaper too. Personally I don't want to make eating a meal complicated for my dogs. Dinner is and should be one of the highlights of a dog's day, as far as I am concerned. I want them to relax, eat and enjoy what they have eaten, but this is just a personal matter. I would be so annoyed if someone put my main meal in front of me but I had to work out how to get at it, wouldn't you? There is a definite place for slow feeding balls/bowls etc., for stimulating and tiring over active or bored dogs, but as for slowing feeding down, I prefer to use a less strenuous method for these dogs at their normal meal time.

Dogs who are greedy eaters may have a tendency to become aggressive feeders, because of the need to keep it to themselves. I have a sheep dog x named Beanie, when she came into our home at six-months old, she was a dog who had received none of the early stimulus we have spoken about in this book. She had many, many issues, including fear and aggression to name but two.

She would have eaten not only the dinner at speed, but anyone who got too close, man or beast. Amongst other methods to deal with her aggression, I used the lap tray method and over time she realised there was nothing to panic about and that no one was coming to take her food. She eats from a normal bowl now and she no longer attacks anyone in the vicinity of her food, which is always a huge relief to those who live with her.

Fussy feeders
Fussy feeders, is there such a thing? These are the dogs who people refer to as not being interested in food, or can't seem to be bothered eating, or only like certain things. This is not a natural behaviour for dogs and is definitely a learnt one by how the dog is raised.

Some people just love to spoil their dogs, they love to cook for them and give them complete variety in what they eat. In my personal experience, as I have already mentioned, there is nothing wrong with adding some variety to your dog's main meal, but adding it too the main diet is the key, not giving it instead of their usual meal. If you start alternating what you feed your dog, he will quickly become choosy and start to turn her nose up at what you are feeding her.

Whatever variety you want to feed her, you must add it and mix it well with her normal meal. This makes the normal meal much more exciting to eat.

I am sure we would all agree, that dogs are not stupid, they know the difference between one type of food and the other, they know what they like and what they don't. How you rear them and how you feed them is crucial to keeping a healthy mental attitude to eating as well as keeping them physically healthy.

If you feed your dog, plain dog kibble in the morning and then feed him dog kibble and meat in the evening, it won't take long before he starts to leave the morning feed as it just isn't as palatable or as interesting as the evening feed. If you are feeding him twice a day, make both meals the same, so that he doesn't pick and choose which he eats.

Ace's Top Tip

If your puppy is leaving food or refusing to eat, it is most likely not hungry rather than not liking it. So trying cutting back, rather than trying something new. If in doubt about your pup not eating, seek veterinary advice.

Aggressive feeders

Sometimes dogs see the need to defend what is theirs in the bowl by displaying aggression. This can come in the form of growling, snarling, tensing up when approached, snapping and in the worst case scenario biting or even attacking. Often this behaviour starts within the litter when puppies feel the need to fight for food when they are being weaned. When I have had a litter, I make sure that the puppies always have more food than they can eat when they are being weaned, I need them to walk away knowing there is always more than enough. This helps prevent the need for squabbling over food. Although sometimes there are personalities that just have to exert themselves.

Puppy table manners

The last litter of Tibetan puppies I had, there was one such puppy, every time feed time would start, if one of the other puppies got too close to where he was eating, he would snarl and snap, he was the only puppy with this attitude. I saw it as my job to stop this behaviour in order that he had let go of this attitude to food, before he went to his new home. So here are the steps I took to teach him table manners.

Step 1 – Meal one. Every time he tensed or made a sound I would touch him on the back, the first couple of times I done this, it startled him and he left the meal refusing to eat. I was not bothered as I needed him to know that his behaviour was unacceptable and there was a bigger dog at the table, (me) who was not prepared to accept his objections. I should add, he returned to the bowl and ate when everyone else had finished.

Step 2 – Meal two. Again he snarled, I touched him and he shot round looked at me and continued eating without a sound.

Step 3 – Meal three. As he approached the bowl he looked straight up at me, rather sheepishly, which was a good sign as I knew he was conscious of controlling his behaviour around me.

Step 4 – Further meals. I always stayed present at meal times, to make sure that he did not regress and I am pleased to say, he never once growled or tensed after that and he showed a positive relaxed attitude to eating.

So what this puppy learnt was a consequence for the action and an objection to his assertiveness. This lesson will have stood this puppy in good stead for later in life and I was fortunate to have contact with the owners through puppy classes, who reported that they had never witnessed any of this behaviour.

Preventing your puppy from becoming aggressive over food

Make sure puppy isn't hungry, the hungrier they are the more they will scoff and defend what they have got.

Feed frequently – 4 times a day from 8 to 12 weeks, then drop to 3 meals until approximately 4 to 5 months. Then you can drop to 2 at approximately 6 months and stick with 2 meals a day, it is better for the dog's digestion than eating 1 large meal. It's also a whole lot less hours that the pup has to go without food.

Extremely important is to stay present while your dog is eating. In fact, hold the bowl while your dog feeds. Keep your hand on the bowl the whole time she is eating, you can even lift some of the food and hand it to her. This will teach her that all food comes from you and you are not there to steal the food. It is too easy to throw a bowl of food at the dog, because you are busy and come back and pick up the empty bowl. Take the time to share in your dog's meal time, this will be valuable time spent at your dog's table. This will help keep a good healthy association to you being present around his food.

I have 6 dogs, feeding time takes approximately ½ hour to 40 minutes from start to finish, I stay with them throughout this special time.

It is important if you have children that they are encouraged to be present too, but they must remain calm and quiet to create a peaceful atmosphere for your dog eating. Encourage them to keep a hand on the puppies bowl, or hold the bowl while she eats. You must remain present at all times to ensure your child gets this right and doesn't upset the puppy.

Should dogs graze?

Some dog food companies recommend leaving your dog constant access to their dry food, this is what I call grazing and in my opinion this is never a good practice and confuses the mind of the dog.

Dogs are not grazers, cows are grazers. The dog's genetics tells them when they see food they should eat it or lose it. It is not good to have a bowl of food on the floor all day, your puppy will soon become bored with it and there is nothing exciting to look forward to, particularly when the next meal of the day is the same. I always feel so sorry for dogs when their owners tell me they feed by this method. I wouldn't want to eat the same meal every day, all day, which is effectively what is happening. Your dog's dinner should be a highlight of the day.

The eat it or lose it rule, creates a healthy mind set to food and stops problems from developing further down the line. If your puppy where in a pack of dogs or in her litter still and she didn't eat her food, another dog would come along and eat it for her. This is what she understands, she has no concept of, 'I don't like that, and I would like something else please'. Humans create this attitude, by offering an alternative every time the dog doesn't feel like eating.

When you put a meal down for your puppy, give her 5 minutes to decide if she is going to eat it, if she walks away and doesn't want it, remove it straight away. Do not allow her to pick and choose when to eat. In removing the food, you are acting as the other dog in the pack. She will learn quickly the eat it or lose it rule. Unless your puppy is ill, if she walks away from the food she is probably not hungry and having more than enough to eat.

Summary - preventing fussy eaters

o   Stick with the programme – whatever food your puppy comes with, stick with it until she is settled and adjusted to your environment. Introduce food changes gradually to avoid upset stomachs.
o   Do not chop and change what you are going to feed. This confuses your puppy and can make for a very unsettled puppy.
o   Always wet puppy meal, whatever swelling it does when wet, should be done before it hits your puppy's tummy.
o   Never leave food down. If she walks away from it, take it away. She is not hungry and doesn't want it. Offer her nothing until the next meal time.

o   Any leftovers or other food being offered to her, should be added to her dog meal, not given instead off. Mix it well so that she can't pick it out.

How much food should you feed your puppy?

How much you feed your puppy is the key to how they continue to eat. While I said earlier that I like a puppy to be well fed and to not feel hungry after she has eaten, there are occasions when you might need to cut back on what your puppy is eating, if she is refusing food.

Assuming your puppy is fit and healthy, if your puppy starts to leave or refuse food, they are probably having too much, look at how much your puppy has left and deduct this amount from future meals. It is better to encourage your puppy to leave a clean bowl than to leave food behind. It is very rare that a puppy will over eat, except perhaps if it is a Labrador, they really don't have an 'I am full' switch, although I am sure there is always the exception to the rule.

Most puppies start to leave food when they have left their litter. This is because there is no competition for the food and they know there is a constant supply, particularly as many first time owners leave them access to food constantly.

I like to keep my dog's dinners exciting. Dogs look forward to their dinner time and therefore it should be something they want to eat and that I have put sometime into preparing for them. I feed a high quality complete dry food that allows for me to add 25% of whatever I want to it, allowing my dog to receive a variety of ingredients. This means whatever I am cooking, I can cook a little extra and add it to their meal, this brings exciting smells to the dinner table for my dogs and the complete meal ensures they are getting everything they need and more.

08 Toilet Training Made Simple

In this chapter
*   How to have a clean puppy in super quick time
*   It comes with being a puppy
*   Designating the right toilet area
*   How to recognise the signs that your pup needs the toilet?
*   Toilet training summary
*   Trouble shooting — what to do if she won't go?

So far, we have looked at den training and feeding and for me the next most important stage to living happily with our puppy is Toilet Training. For me toilet training should never be an issue, unless of course you are dealing with a puppy who suffers with submissive urination, now that is a whole other matter, which we will deal with later. The aim of my toilet training method, is to have the puppy clean in the shortest time possible. Follow this method and it is full proof for delivering on this.

The crate-den is the first stage in dealing with this. You should now be well underway with crate training, so let us take a detailed look at toilet training and how to master it in the shortest time possible.

How to have a clean puppy in super-quick time
The best I can hope for is that you are reading this book before getting your pup, second best would be that you are reading it shortly after getting your puppy.

Waking every morning to a wet and smelly mess is no fun for anyone. You will no doubt have been given copious amounts of advice on what is best. If you have considered paper training, puppy pad training, leaving the door open so he can come and go when he needs to. STOP! Forget all of those methods because they can each come with their own problems, depending upon how your dog interprets what you are teaching.

75

Methods past and present

The following description of a toilet training method, is perhaps the most popular method handed down over the years, I myself used this method in my early days. Some may still use this method, but I want to show you that there is a better way to tackle this important matter.

All stress ends here for you and your puppy. This particular toilet training routine has been tried and tested for more than 20 years without failure. Following this method, you will have a clean dog in the shortest possible time. The only time I consider putting newspaper down for a puppy to toilet is, if you have to leave her at home for a period of time on her own, where she can't be crated, but I would still suggest newspaper in this instance and definitely not puppy pads.

Mr Tibs' Training Tip

Newspaper and puppy pad training, is not a method I recommend.

This method involved placing paper on the floor where puppy has access to it. The area is gradually decreased in size, moving the paper gradually towards the door, it is hoped that the puppy will gradually follow the paper towards the door to the outside area, and learn that this is where he is supposed to toilet. In recent years the newspaper has been substituted for puppy pads, these are rather like a baby's diaper, holding more urine and keeping the floor cleaner. These can prove a disaster in toilet training don't do it, resist the urge.

Newspaper and pad training often have the opposite effect to what people are lead to believe they will have. These methods give your dog permission to toilet indoors, the complete opposite of what you are hoping to achieve. They should only be used as a last resort, if you can't be around to put your puppy out. If this is a regular occurrence then perhaps you should be asking yourself the question, is the timing right for you to own a dog who has needs that need to be met.

Puppy Training Pads are a big NO-NO In my training, the only good use I have found for them is in the whelping box when the bitch is giving birth and for keeping the litter box clean in the early days. Or for dogs who are incontinent.

Puppy training pads are used pretty much the same as newspaper, except that they offer more padding for her to feel comfortable about weeing on, they soak up the wee and your puppy learns if she targets something thick she doesn't get wet feet, this is never a good thing, and often leads to the puppy targeting a rug, carpet or door mat as a preferable area to avoid having to deal with the mess.

We have already established the crate den as our preferred method, if however, you have chosen to go for a room with a normal dog bed for puppy, or even the pen, then Toilet training will take a bit longer in the beginning, as your puppy has the freedom to toilet in this area when it suits her and has no need to learn to hold it or to tell you she needs to go. She will over time get the idea, but this often takes longer and you may want to put something down in one corner for her to target toileting in case you don't get to her in time to get her outside.

If you have decided to go for the crate and have established that it is the right size, then we are on the road to fast track toilet training. Refer back to Crate-Den training if you are uncertain about any aspect.

It comes with being a puppy

I think I am safe in saying whenever a puppy arrives in a new home, we all expect a certain amount of change and a little chaos to take place as everything seems to centre around the new arrival. It also goes without saying that we all know a certain amount of weeing and pooping is to be expected on a regular daily basis, this is normal, all puppies have to learn how to hold their bladder and bowel. It is our job to teach them when and where to go to the toilet.

Your pup does not need to make a mess around the house, it should not be possible for your pup to wander around the house and toilet where she chooses. Permitting this to a happen, can set up big problems for the future. Precautions must be put in place to prevent this from the beginning.

Let me tell you about puppy training pads

The biggest challenge in toilet training your puppy, is commitment from YOU the owner. The biggest failure in toilet training is the dog being left to toilet without supervision, or the latest fad as described above, is providing the dog with puppy training pads, so that it has the option to choose whether to toilet indoors if it needs to in an emergency.

I am screeching you to a halt right there. I can hear those of you who have pad trained a puppy before saying, 'Well it worked for me, I didn't have a problem with it'. Then good for you and I am pleased for you, but for every one person who says puppy pads where successful, I could show you at least four or five that were not successful. Psychologically, this procedure is confusing for the dog and as a behaviourist and a dog trainer, I personally wish they had never been invented.

Putting anything on the floor and allowing your puppy to toilet on it gives your puppy permission to use the indoors as a toilet area, let alone putting a cushion on the floor, i.e. a puppy pad, which means the wee soaks in instantly, your pup never experiences wet feet and neither has she had to paddle in it, what luxury. As your pup grows, the chances of her checking out your rug or door mat for toileting on becomes a very high possibility, as it is no different at all to a pad. It provides the same comfort to do the deed and it is flat lying on the floor, beckoning to be toileted on.

I have seen many puppies regress back to toileting indoors around 6 to 8 months of age, who were raised on puppy pads. **Don't Do It**. Resist the urge and make the effort to toilet your dog's outside regularly and they will not only be clean quickly, they will be reliable for life in holding and controlling their bladder and bowel, unless they are ill of course.

I credit a lot of my success in toilet training with the fact that the dog is accompanied to the toilet at all times, until they know exactly what is expected of them. This may be a year, or it may be shorter. I prefer to observe my dogs going to the toilet, as I know then, If they have gone and done the deed and if there is an upset tummy you can detect it straight away. It also avoids accidents, as you know your puppy definitely went before allowing them freedom indoors.

Through the years that I have worked as an Applied Animal Behaviourist, I had the pleasure of Pre–Vaccination Puppy Training with hundreds of puppies, in their homes. Most people accept that a little mess is normal, as puppies can't help themselves, right? WRONG! Your' puppy may need to toilet frequently, but they do not need to toilet in the home at all.

'Accidents', in the home happen because 'you' allow them to, and you aren't being consistent enough in taking puppy out regularly. Accept that they are your mistakes and move on. Mistakes are fine, as long as they aren't allowed to keep repeating.

Designating the right toilet area

Hopefully you will have thought it through, before getting your puppy, where you want her to toilet, however if you haven't got a preferred toilet area, choose one now and stick to it. My dog's toilet on concrete only at home, I have worked with many people who had a grass only area available to them, but they were still able to designate a specific area of the garden, that way preventing the loss of your complete lawn, and avoiding stepping in those missed accidents, particularly if you have children.

Concrete versus grass

Concrete is the ideal surface, from a cleanliness and hygiene point of view. The mess is easily picked up and the area scrubbed down, which keeps smells down and stops your lawn from turning brown. It's also easier to tell if your dog has gone or not.

If a dog is taught to toilet on concrete they will go anywhere you want them to, if they are raised toileting on grass, this can make it difficult if your faced with a situation where there is no grass available or they cannot go on the grass.

It also means you can tell if your dog is ill, as you can see on the concrete what's in her stools and the colour of her wee, if there are any problems.

Grass: A dog taught to go on grass will most likely only ever go on grass, and will refuse to go if not given access to grass. This can make things difficult if you go on holiday, and there isn't any grass available, particularly when travelling.

It's hard to tell on grass whether there are any problems, as it soaks into the grass almost immediately. You will also have no lawn to speak of in a very short space of time. Urine will turn the grass brown as it burns the grass.

If your dog shares the lawn with your children for playing, you will need to do poo patrol before the children are allowed to play out, quite frustrating when the children want to go play 'now', if you don't find the poo now, you can be sure your children will find it.

If you have no concrete, then you could consider laying a few paving stones in a corner, or some gravel for her to toilet on. It's not hard to do and is fairly inexpensive.

Location of the toilet area
More often than not when I do a home visit the owner has chosen as their pup's toilet area a spot at the back of the garden, away from the house. I fully understand the thinking, that they don't want poo and wee where they are going to be having their summer bar-b-ques, however the back of the garden is really not a good idea and once I explain it, to people you can see that light bulb moment where they realise it just is not a good idea or mores to the point the suggestion I give them is a better one.

A toilet area at the far end of the garden:
* Your pup will have to hold what she needs to do for a longer time until she reaches the area.
* You will need to carry her to the area for a longer time to prevent her toileting where you don't want it.

- You will have to make trips across the garden to clean the area, multiple times in the day, whatever the weather.
- In winter, your dog is going to bring in all the mud of the garden since she has to cross it twice just to toilet.
- Did your dog actually go when she went to the end of the garden? How will you know when you can't see?
- How will you know if she has diarrhoea if you can't see what she's doing? Or blood in her urine? Will you always accompany her to the bottom of the garden?

Toileting in a small area close to the house on concrete far outweighs any other area, in its practicalities. Even if you have to make a small fenced off area, for your pup to contain where they go.

Recognising the signs that your pup needs the toilet

Eating, **sleeping** and **playing**, all key trigger points for needing to toilet.

When they eat - Although, with some dogs the time varies on this one, but generally, after you have fed her, allow her time to have a drink if she wants one, and then guide her straight to the toilet area and wait.

When they wake from sleeping. Every time your puppy goes to sleep and wakes up, she will **without a doubt** need to wee. Many will do it as soon as they wake; your job is to get her to the toilet area as soon as possible.

When they have played. If you are playing with puppy and she suddenly loses interest and starts to wander away, direct her immediately to your designated toilet area and wait. Sometimes puppies dart away really quickly mid game as they suddenly realise they need the loo, it's a bit like the child who leaves it to the last minute.

In the first week or two carry your puppy to the toilet as they probably won't make the distance. There is plenty of time to teach them to follow you outside but for now carry her so that mistakes don't occur on the way.

Teaching your dog to toilet on Cue is so easy to teach and a brilliant tool once the dog understands it. When she is actually squatting to wee or poo, (Not Before) introduce a cue word or phrase like, 'Go Busy' or 'Be Quick', while she is still doing it. This way she will quickly associate the cue with the action. Tell her she is a good girl at the time she is doing her business, but be calm with your praise in case you distract her and she doesn't complete the job.

When she has finished make a big fuss of her, and if it's appropriate let her go play or investigate for a few minutes either inside or outside. It won't take long before she catches on that if she toilets quickly, she gets some freedom and to come back indoors. However be aware that some dogs occasionally are so excited that they know they are going to get freedom to play, they don't do all they need to and if this happens they will finish it when you set them free inside. If this happens return her immediately to the toilet area for a couple of minutes to make your point that she can only toilet where you want her to, even if she finished it indoors.

Eventually when you take her out and say the cue word or phrase you have chosen. E.g., 'Go Busy', she will immediately switch her

mind to finding a suitable spot for toileting. As soon as she obliges, tell her good girl and reward her with praise, but not treats.

Ace's Top Tip
Never allow your dog to have the run of the house until she is completely toilet trained. Toilet accidents indoors become bad habits very quickly.

The more frequently she is put outdoors to toilet, the faster she will learn what it is you expect her to do. However, if you are putting her out too often, say every half hour to an hour, she may not need to go and this equally can mean things take longer to connect for her. Make a note for a few days every time she wees and every time she poos to get an idea or her pattern, then you can pre-empt when she will need to go and take her out just before the time.

Mr Tibs' Training Tip

Consider her mistakes as your mistakes, she only toilets indoors because you allow it to happen.

Toilet Training Summary

1. Confine your dog to a secure area of the house when you can't watch her, never leave her unattended. The kitchen and preferably within her own den will restrict her movements and encourage her to hold onto what she needs to do.
2. If she is restricted, she will call you when she needs to go to avoid soiling her bed.
3. When you take her to the toilet stay with her until she goes. (Even if it's wet, windy or snowing!). She will cry and become distracted if you leave her alone and you won't know if she's been.
4. When she squats to perform give her a cue, "GO BUSY", or "BE QUICK". Only say the cue 'as she is actually toileting' and praise with "Good Boy/Girl"!
5. When she has done her business outdoors, reward her by giving her freedom to play in the house or a run in the garden, Do Not reward her with food.
6. If while she is playing with you in the house, she decides to toilet, hurry straight to her, clapping your hands at her at the same time making a loud growling noise, to distract her from what she is doing, pick her up and take her straight to her toilet area and hopefully you will have stopped her mid flow and she will finish it off in her toilet area. Even if she had already finished it indoors, it is important that you put her into the toilet area that you have created for her for a few moments, to make the point, that this is where that behaviour should take place. Be consistent, she will get the message, much quicker than you will imagine.
7. The procedure described in no 6, should be used if she is playing in your garden with you and she decides to toilet, take her straight to her toilet area, every time. She will eventually leave

the garden and head for there, every time she has the urge to toilet when playing. This means you and your family get to enjoy your garden and your dog gets to share it with you, but doesn't get to own it or make it their own.

What to do if your dog will not toilet when you take her outside

For this method of toilet training to succeed, the discipline must be in the commitment from 'you' to follow through and not allow your pup to make mistakes. A favourite problem I hear from people is,

'I take the puppy outside and stand and wait, and wait, and wait some more. I have waited up to 40 minutes and she does nothing, I bring her inside and within two minutes of being inside, she has done a wee, what do I do?'

I suggest you try the following

1. When you are standing outside with your pup, if she just sits by your feet, then start to move around the toilet area. She will most likely follow you. Movement will be more likely to stimulate her to go. Do not talk to her. Talking will distract her.
2. If she still doesn't go, bring her back indoors and restrict all freedom of movement around the house when you bring her in. Do not let her walk around, at all. Hold her in your arms, if she is small enough or keep her on a lead by your side or you can even put her in her crate-den for 5 minutes (if you are sure she won't toilet in it), but if you opt for crating her, do not wander off and leave her in it as she is certain to be forced to toilet in it if you disappear. When she gets fidgety or whines, take her outside again.
3. Do not tell your dog off or get angry, remain calm at all times and be patient.
4. Unless you catch your dog in the act of soiling in the house there is absolutely no point in telling her off. In fact, you will most definitely make matters worse, as she will become worried when you go out that you are going to tell her off when you return home, this will most likely cause her to wee or poo due to stress.

09 Night-Time Toilet Training

In his chapter
- Pros and Con's
- Step-by-step to a silent night

Pros and Con's

I have given night time toilet training a small chapter of its own, as it is such an important aspect to conquer. Not only does this method give you clean nights, but it also gives you quiet stress free nights, so the whole family gets to sleep with no wailing stressed out puppy.

This method of night toilet training is by far the best both in speed and in consistency that I have worked with. It involves commitment from you the owner perhaps even a little more than the daytime training. This method may not suit everyone, but I would suggest you weigh up all pros and cons, before discounting it.

Pros:
- No wee and poo all over your floor and worse still on your puppy's feet as he walked through it in the night.
- No floors to scrub clean every morning.
- No smell
- No having to be up before everyone else, so the floors can be cleaned.
- Your puppy will be clean in the shortest possible time.
- No crying or screaming puppy keeping you, your family and worse still your neighbours awake. She won't cry because she's with you, this is a wonderful method of helping your puppy to settle in quickly, as all separation problems are solved, and no anxiety caused to your puppy.

Cons:

- Yes, you will have disturbed sleep in the night for a short period of time.
- Yes, you will feel tired the next day.
- Your puppy will sleep in your bedroom or you in her room for a short time.
- I know immediately, that many of you reading this who have had any experience of reading about dog training, will be thinking 'it's not good to have your dog in your bedroom and he's always going to want to be there'. This is not the case, this programme is designed to prevent this from happening.
- If you have a partner who is a light sleeper and your moving around in the night may cause disturbance, then it may be a good idea to sleep with puppy in another room or even bed down on the couch for a few nights.

As I mentioned in the den training section, the den you have chosen for your dog should be just big enough for her to stand up, turn round and lie down comfortably.

If like most people, you have bought a den that will last her into adulthood; you may need to insert a divider to make the living space smaller, so that it is much smaller for night time and when she is left alone. The divider is left in place, until your pup has grown a bit bigger and no longer has space to toilet at one end, or until she has learnt to ask to go out. I divide the den by either putting in a cardboard box or a plastic storage box, big enough to fill the back part of the den or apiece of ply drilled with holes and cable tied does the job well.

Many dog crates now come with dividers which you can fit to suit your dog. The bedding then goes in front of the divider or in one side, depending upon the layout of your crate. If you don't put a divider in and the cage is too big, she will be tempted to use one end as her toilet, as it will still have adequate space to sleep away from it. This will defeat the object. The idea is to create a small enough space that your pup will cry to tell you when she needs to toilet. Your pup won't want to soil her bed if she can help it. Toileting in her bed, will cause her undue distress, dogs will never soil their bed area, unless something has gone wrong in their development or training process. Many pups will not even soil near to it, if raised properly. If left with no option but to soil where she sleeps, this would be cruel and may result in a dog with serious toileting issues.

Step-by-step to a silent night

By making the den sleeping area much smaller, your puppy will become very restless when she wakes, she will cry to get your attention and to let you know she needs to get out away from her bed to toilet.

- Your puppy will have to sleep close to you in her crate-den so that you can hear her cry. I find that right next to my bed at my head end, makes certain I hear her when she moans. Do not be tempted to leave puppy downstairs and assume you will hear her, this will be disastrous if you don't get to her quickly enough. All puppies vary as to how much effort they make to let you know. Some barely make a whimper, but fidget around, while others scream like they are being murdered.
- When your puppy cries it is important that you take her out as soon as you hear her whimper.

IMPORTANT: I cannot stress it enough, under no circumstances should your puppy be forced to toilet in her bed, this will not only cause complications in your training, but it is also cruel as a dog will normally not soil where she sleeps and this will cause undue stress.

- When you pick your puppy up in the night, do not stimulate her with lots of conversation and petting, she needs to know this is night time, not play time, just as you would with a human baby. That way she will be willing to go back to bed.
- Calmly take her to the toilet area and remain quiet. If you're anything like me in the middle of the night that's all you will want to do anyway.
- As soon as she has done everything you think she needs to (remember puppies usually poop in the middle of the night so you will have to allow extra time for her to do everything) pick her up and take her straight back to bed.

- Put her into her den, close the door and turn the light out. She may complain for a minute or two but she will settle again. I find it best to tap on the cage if puppy cries, that way they know you are still there, even though they can't see you. I find they seem to settle quicker once they are aware of your presence.
- Your puppy will wake you as often as she needs to toilet, but this will depend on the individual dog and how good their bladder and bowel control is.
- You must never, ever show your displeasure at being woken up, no matter how rough you may feel.
- Remember this will only be for a few nights, so don't despair. Depending on your puppy, will depend on how long it takes for her to sleep all night. Once your puppy is sleeping all night, (and this may happen as early as the 3rd or 4th night, however don't rush things until you know for certain), the process of moving her from your bedroom can begin.

Remember: that it is not unusual for a puppy in her new home to sleep soundly all night on the first and maybe even the second night. So make the most of it as the protests usually begin after this.

- Once your puppy is now sleeping through the night without waking for toileting, it is now time to start relocating her to the kitchen or other chosen spot away from your bedroom. You can do a weaning process with this by first moving the crate outside your bedroom door and then over a week, moving it further away.
- When I first put my puppies back in the kitchen, I use a baby monitor just in case she decides she needs to toilet. This sometimes happens once or twice as they just need to know that you are still there and it's important that you respond to her straight away.
- If you can't afford a baby monitor then keep her with you a while longer, or keep her outside your bedroom for a while longer until you are certain she is no longer needing you in the night.

For me, the small price you pay of being woken in the night is a relaxed puppy, a clean house and a family well slept— albeit you may be a little tired. It won't last long, promise!

10 Handling and Grooming

In this chapter

- Handling + Grooming = Bonding
- Why is handling and grooming so important at this age?
- Handling vs cuddling
- When should you groom your pup?
- How to groom for the best results

Handling + Grooming = Bonding & Trust & Good Hygiene

For me, this is one of the most vital parts of training with all dogs and one of the least carried out in the early days, until it's needed of course, or until there is a problem.

I consider handling and grooming to be one of the most overlooked aspects of training. There are few Dog training Schools that offer this area of training as an essential exercise, to forming a strong bond and as a means to preventing problems from developing. Although the Kennel Club Good Citizen Scheme asks for it as part of the criteria for being certificated, perhaps a good reason for seeking out such a club.

In my experience, handling and grooming encourages the bond and respect, between owner and pup that is needed for the future to be built on a mutual understanding between the two. I consider it such an important element, that I dedicate at least one whole session in each of my training courses to it. Each owner in turn will handle his or her own dog on a table or surface applicable to their dog, and I will look at any problems they may have or are likely to encounter at home.

Why is handling and grooming so important at this early age?

Within a pack it would be considered the pack-leaders right to groom another pack member or to be groomed by another pack member when he or she chooses to do so.

In my years as a dog trainer, most of the problems that people have come to me with, when questioned, most would struggle with some aspect of handling or grooming their dog. As a result of this, it is one of the key questions I ask in my consultation, "Will your dog let you groom and handle every aspect of his body without a struggle?"

If your dog will accept this in its entirety with no, no go areas, then there is a good chance you will be able to train her, as there may already be a relationship of respect and trust there, with the exception of some fine tuning that you may need taken care of.

Before grooming can take place it is important that your puppy accepts being handled and learns to keep still. Here is an exercise that is great for teaching puppy to be calm and relax when gentle restraint is put on them. This exercise needs to be done as early as possible in the puppy's development, or you may end up with a frantic irate puppy who doesn't accept restraint lightly.

Handling vs cuddling

Start handling your puppy from day one, and by handling I don't mean just cuddling, 'as important as it is'. It is important to teach your puppy the importance of keeping still when you need to hold her to examine her, treat her or groom her.

This exercise you are going to teach your puppy, is not the same as cuddling your puppy, this handling is a restraint hold, to teach your puppy how to relax and trust you when you restrain her.

1. Practice picking your pup up and just hold her securely in your arms, against your body. If she struggles or complains, keep hold until she stops. As soon as she relaxes let your hands caress her and then set her free.

Note: Some puppies may scream, growl, and fight as though their life depends upon getting free, this is determined very much by the personality of each individual puppy. The more determined or assertive the puppy, the more fuss they will create. Do not stress about this, remember you are only holding her and no harm can come to her. Being held is an essential exercise. Do not let go until she has stopped struggling and relaxed.

2. This handling is essential particularly for visiting the vet or groomer in the future. Once your puppy has accepted this, she will not complain about having to be restrained in any situation and she will trust you to tend to her when needed.
3. This handling is the first step in communicating to your puppy that you are her protector and her leader and she can trust you. Practice this exercise regularly.
4. This handling should not be used as a punishment; it is merely an exercise just like teaching sit or down.
5. Do not practice this exercise when the puppy is very excited and lively. This is best tackled when she is a little tired.

Remember: Never put a struggling puppy down, putting her down will teach her that protesting is a way to get what she wants.

Helping your pup to enjoy grooming

When should you groom your pup?
o   In the early days, every day for five minutes will help establish a pattern quickly.

Who should groom the pup?
o   Every member of the family should take it in turn to handle and groom the dog. This includes the children, if they are to receive respect from the dog. Children should always be supervised during sessions with the dog.

Which dogs need grooming?
o   All dogs should be groomed. Grooming is not limited to those dogs that have long coats. It is as important for the short-coated breeds. It gives you the opportunity to do a daily health check on your dog, as dogs often develop skin rashes or lumps without us noticing until suddenly there is a skin infection or hair loss.

My dog will have long hair, what should I know?
o   If you have chosen a breed that will have a long, thick coat like my breed, the Tibetan Terrier, in order to keep this coat you will need to groom your dog very, very regularly.
o   Your dog needs to be taught to keep still while she is young and the coat is short, this makes it easier to deal with grooming sessions, when the coat begins to grow.
o   Do not wait until the dog has a long coat, to groom her or she will be very reluctant to comply with your requests and grooming sessions will not be a pleasant experience.

How do I beginning grooming my puppy?
o   Practice picking your puppy and just setting her on the work surface with a few tasty treats.
o   Do this regularly until she is looking forward to being placed on the table. (See the following section for full details)

How to groom for best results

1.   Choose a suitable work surface and put a non-slip mat (a bath mat or car mat) on it.
2.   Make your surface against a wall if possible. This means one side is protected preventing your dog from jumping off. I.e. a kitchen work surface or in the garage or utility room it could be the top of your washing mashing etc.

You can also buy a purpose made grooming table, which will last forever and are fairly inexpensive.

Grooming table

3.   If you go for a do it yourself one, put an 'eye-hook' in the wall so that you can attach her lead to it, this enables you to have both hands free for working on the dog rather than having to hold her in place on the table.
4.   Make sure you have all your grooming equipment at hand before placing your dog on the surface. *(NEVER LEAVE YOUR DOG FOR A SECOND ON ANY SURFACE,* many dogs have no awareness that they are tethered and will attempt to jump whether attached by a lead or not, the results could spell disaster.)

5. Handle your dog firmly and confidently checking her ears, eyes, teeth, paws and tail-end for anything unusual.
6. Run your fingers over the skin feeling for anything unusual, lift the coat the wrong way and check for signs of fleas. (Tiny specks of black dirt may be flea droppings.
7. To test for flea droppings, take a piece of damp cotton wool and dab the dirt, if it is flea dirt it will dissolve to a red brown colour which is the dried blood of the flea faeces).

Points 5 and 6 need to be carried out regularly before you need to even brush your pup. This will help your pup to adjust to just having hands on her and not running around biting.

Do not miss out the grooming exercise because your puppy doesn't need it right now, it does not matter whether it is a Jack Russell, Labrador or a Tibetan Terrier, start the handling and grooming process now. It will highlight and particular areas your pup may object to and you can do something about it before it gets out of hand.

It will also allow you to do a daily health exam on your puppy, so that any problems are identified early. Getting to know your dog's body and what is normal for her could save her life and save on huge vet bills.

Remember your dog is developing and maturing right up until she is about 2 or 3 years old, other breeds like the German shepherd are not mature until around 4 years. For this reason, it is important that you keep up with the handling and grooming, so that any changes in attitude your' dog may be developing, don't pass you by and end up a problem.

Remember too, that if your dog is a breed which is going to go to a groomer regularly, it is not good enough that you leave all the work to them. You must do the homework, so that your dog behaves for the groomer or you can expect to pay a higher bill.

My favourite brushes

Bass Palm Brush or straight palm brush and the double headed matt zapper.

**My favourite, a
horse mane comb**

11 Introducing your Pup to the World

In this Chapter

Getting to know your vet

Your pup has just been taken away from her mum, spent her first night away from her dog family and arrived with a new family she doesn't know or understand. This new family 'You', now has the task of taking her to another strange place, that smells peculiar and the chances are she is there to have her vaccine, a needle stuck in his neck. Ouch and how scary. Sometime later, you may find yourself complaining to the Dog Trainer or Behaviourist, "my dog absolutely hates the vet", and together you now have the task of trying to understand why!

It doesn't have to be like that. A little advanced thinking and planning can make all the difference.

Give your pup a day or two to get to know you. Puppies vary a great deal as to how quickly they settle down. Many arrive in their home and move in making it their own almost instantly, others need time to feel confident and relax with you, some find the whole experience traumatic and they may even develop an upset tummy, and worse even a temperature to go with it etc.

Fortunately, there are not that many like this, but it does happen. If the breeder of your puppy is anything like me, they will have asked that you take your puppy to visit the vet of your choice within a 48 or 72-hour period, for an independent health check.

Ideally **do not** make this first visit to the vet, the one where your puppy receives her first vaccine.

Creating a positive experience for your pup

- *Your first visit to the vet* – Make an appointment for a social visit to meet the vet and the practice staff. This visit is important to let them meet your pup, say hello and generally just check her over, but keeping everything positive. This should be a relaxed and enjoyable experience.
- Your Vet may give your puppy a yeast tablet or similar food-treat to chew on to help her relax, however take some tasty treat with you just in case, to help puppy associate the new environment with something positive.
- I cannot stress enough Do Not have your puppy 'vaccinated' on this trip; make another appointment for another time, even a day or two later. Believe me it is well worth spending the little time and extra money, to create a lifetime of happy, stress-free vet trips for your pup.
- *Your second visit to the vet* – When taking her back for her vaccination take some extra treats with you to help her relax on the table during the vaccination, again your Vet will probably give her a treat, to help take her mind of things, but be prepared just in case.
- My puppies have never been aware of the needle being administered because of the care being shown to them. Remember to gently rub the spot where the needle has been administered, to prevent swelling from the vaccine afterwards and minimise the stinging. Some pup's panic a few seconds after the shot because of this, rubbing can help alleviate this.
- Keep gently rubbing while your pup is on the table and your vet is finishing of the details and giving you all relevant information, this will help in relaxing the muscle, preventing the huge swelling that can happen, which can be quite tender for a few days after for the pup.

During this period of waiting for puppy to be fully covered from the life threatening diseases, there is a lot you can do to safely prepare her for the great big world and all that comes with it.

A lot of new puppy owners when told, they must not take their pup out until one week after their second vaccine, take it very literally.

This does not mean that your pup cannot go in your garden to toilet. Of course puppy must toilet outdoors from the moment you bring her home, if you are to prevent problems from arising. Start as you mean to go on.

What is socialisation?

Many dog owners believe that puppy classes are the answer to their dog's socialisation. Many are shocked that their adult dog has developed aggression, given that they attended puppy socialisation classes. The truth is that the, puppy socialisation class probably provides your pup with about 5% of the socialisation they need. It is great that more owners are aware of the importance of socialisation, but there is far more to it than simply 'puppy socialisation classes'.

Puppy classes are held in 'one' environment with the same group of people and the same group of dogs for a series of weeks. This is not sufficient to create a well socialised and balanced dog. Socialisation means exposing your pup to a variety of experiences, a variety of different smells and a range of textile surfaces in different locations as safely as is possible, making sure each experience is a positive one especially for the first 13 weeks of her life. Although this is just the beginning and this socialising and adjustment period should continue for at least the first 2 years of her life, while she continues her physical and mental development.

Environmental socialisation

Your puppy can be carried out to meet the outside world for five or ten minutes every day i.e. People, traffic noise, some shops will even let you carry your pup inside. Rest assured that by the time your pup is ready to go walking outdoors she will have adjusted to the hustle and bustle of busy streets, people touching her and doors slamming, traffic passing her etc. Start with a fairly quiet street and hold her while letting her observe the traffic, once she has gotten use to this, take her to a busier road etc. Take her to any shops that will allow you to carry her inside. Banks usually don't have a problem, pet shops and some other retail outlets. It is a great idea to take her to a local school and stand outside with her so that she can acclimatise to the noise and excitement of children. Children cannot resist rushing to a puppy and touching it. Just stand there and let it all happen they will do the work for you in socialising your puppy. Whilst your pup is young, it is crucial that you make the most of this time, you only get one chance at this period, and there is no going back.

Canine socialisation

Remember if you already own a dog make sure he is fully inoculated before your new puppy comes home to your house. Your puppy may be able to go to other people's houses that have dogs that are fully inoculated with a minimum of risk, or even better have one come to yours to visit, to allow your dog to meet a friend. If you're worried about this, ask your vet's advice first but they will most likely tell you no because it's more than they dare do and won't want the responsibility. If the dogs you introduce your puppy to are fully vaccinated this is no greater risk than introducing your puppy to your already resident dog, which goes out walking where other dogs walk. In my opinion, some risks are necessary in order that you can achieve a balanced puppy. Leaving it until your puppy is 12 or 13 weeks could be detrimental to the character of the puppy as she grows into an adult.

Only introduce a dog that you know will be safe with your puppy, this must be a pleasant and positive experience for your puppy. Keep your pup in her crate when first introducing her to another dog, this will allow you to gage the interest of the older dog, before allowing them to meet properly. Better to be safe than sorry, accidents can't be reversed. (For more details on this, check out the section 'introducing puppy to another dog'). Contrary to popular belief, many adult dogs do not like puppies, puppy teeth hurt and they can be quite pushy with no manners. Even the most placid adult dog may prove grumpy when faced with an over exuberant pup. Use the crate to gage this will prevent all accidents from happening.

Ask your Vet also what your area is like with regards to Infections which may affect your puppy, if your area is low risk, it may be that you can walk your pup up and down your road with the minimum of risk to aid getting her use to the lead. However, you will have to weigh up this situation and make your own decision as to how great the risk is. My puppies are always fully lead trained before their vaccinations are complete. You can begin your lead training in your garden too and recall training too, more on that in the training section.

12 Dog Training Schools

In this chapter
- Puppy Parties
- Puppy Training Schools
- How to choose the right training school for you
- Things to watch out for

Puppy Parties

Ask your Vet about a Puppy Party, these are held at the Vets Surgery under more sterile conditions, ideally these sessions should have a Dog Trainer present to give much needed advice, and observe the pup's first interactions both with people and the other pups. The pups should hopefully get to meet the Vet under more 'normal' circumstances. The puppy parties are carried out while puppy is undergoing his vaccination programme. Many vets are holding these now. The puppy gets to meet other people and in particular gets handled by other people including the staff from the practice. However, it might be worth asking whether the vet will be attending. I do wish that more vets would make an effort to attend rather than just the nursing staff, since it is the vet who generally handles the dog.

If your vet doesn't host such a party, perhaps if enough people mention it, your vet may take the initiative to organise one.

Important points to look out for:

- Be sure to check with them that they have a professional trainer present, particularly if the puppies will be let of lead as this type of meeting needs professional monitoring.
- Letting puppies loose in a room to play without the correct supervision is a mistake and can lead to many, many problems. Nothing must go wrong at this stage in your pup's development or it could last a very long time in her memory. I have seen puppies have very poor experiences from these first meetings.

- It is not sufficient that the party is run by practice staff, vets or nurses; while there is no doubt they will be good at what they are trained in, this does not qualify them to recognise potential behaviour problems in the early stages of a puppy's development.

Key elements to the puppy party should be:
- Worming,
- Flea treatment
- Diet
- Vaccinations
- Basic Training/Socialising
- Grooming and Handling
- Playing

Puppy training schools

Start training with your dog from day one. Your Vet may be able to help, as he or she will only recommend training establishments that have a good reputation. Decide what you want from your dog before you go, as this will influence the type of training school you go to, there are various types of dog school. Ask other dog owners, if your vet cannot recommend one, they may have been to one at some time that they can had success with. Recommendation is always a good place to start.

Choosing the right puppy school

You may already be aware of the concept of puppy classes or puppy socialisation groups, but until your pup has completed her vaccination programme, she cannot attend such classes, although it is now becoming popular for some training schools to take puppies after their 1st vaccination. I personally do not feel there is a rush to put puppies into class environments before their vaccine programme has finished. There is plenty of training that you can be getting on with to cover these few weeks.

Puppy Training Classes are very different than the previously mentioned Puppy Parties. However, as a trainer of puppy classes I am only too aware that by the time the puppy has finished her vaccination programme (12/13 wks. or in some cases later) quite a few bad habits have already established themselves and a very important period in the puppy's life may have gone uninfluenced, which is why pre-vac training is so important.

Training MUST start from the moment the dog comes into your home. (Where possible you should inquire about training classes before purchasing your pup, to make sure you have secured a place in the right class for you. This prevents a further delay taking place in your pup's development).

Dog Training schools can vary enormously as to the methods they use. Some can be very competition based, while others are pet owner based, meaning they should be more likely to deal with your daily problems both at home and in training class.

Some questions to ask about the Dog Training School when enquiring

1. Ask if you can visit the class before enrolling.
2. Ask how old the puppies are in the class you attend, and how long they have been coming. This can be a good gauge of how well the training school progresses dogs and owners. A good dog training school will not object. A puppy class should be aged between approximately 12 weeks and no older than 5months, although some schools prefer to mix pups with adults believing this gives a better balance and more natural experience for the pups. However, this type of class needs to be very well controlled and there should be no off lead socialising for safety reasons.
3. How many dogs will be in the class? The smaller the class, the better and no more than 8 to 10, with two trainers present.
4. Are the family allowed to watch the training? Family should be encouraged to at least observe and preferably get involved.

5. Are you and your partner allowed to take it in turn, training the dog in class? – You both have to live with the dog, you should therefore both be able to enjoy the experience of working you're your puppy.

Unfortunately, not all training schools can deal with all requests. You may want to train for Obedience Competitions or Breed Showing or you may just want a well-behaved and socially acceptable dog.

Try to make sure whichever school you go to they are at least, equipped both with time and trainers to deal with any problems you may have.

Try to observe the training methods used

Look at others in the class and talk to them, ask them if they are happy with it and more importantly, is their dog of a standard you would be happy with?

The class should not be overly noisy or too crowded. Too many dogs in a class will lead to a high drop-out rate. The class should be controlled and orderly with no one person or dog dominating the class.

Things to watch out for

- It **should not** be a Free-for-All! Puppies should not be charging around all over the place, with the bullies of the class terrorising those of a more insecure or sensitive nature.
- Lack of Structure to the class
- Owners **are not** being given instruction on how to handle their puppies, or on basic training. If the right advice is not being given, move on find another school.
- Sit, downs and stays are all very important, but a class who deals with handling and grooming is essential in my opinion. At the very least the class should teach you how to hold and restrain

your puppy when necessary without being bitten. An essential exercise that is needed when visiting the vets and groomers.

- It is important that the trainer helps you or gives you advice on problems you are having at home or outside and not just basic training exercises in a class.

Question and Answer

- Time should be allowed for asking your questions and answers given as encouragement.

Age Groups

- If possible, the puppies should **all** be of a similar age.

Equipment

- Toys should be on hand for you and your dog to experience and play with.
- Any training equipment needed or suggested, should be demonstrated. At the very least, collars and leads should available for you to look at; to be sure you are using the right ones for your dog.
-

Ace's Top Tip

The wrong class can be more damaging than good for your puppy—please choose wisely!

13 The Trick is in the Training

In this chapter

- How to nurture natural instinct
- The word association game
- Total Recall through play training
- Whistle training – the emergency
- Puppy-in-the-middle
- Lead walking

How to nurture natural instincts and behaviours

A natural instinct is something that is in-bred, it is something that the dog doesn't have to be taught or think about doing. For example, sitting, lying down, standing up, following, being assertive or submissive, hunting by scent or sight etc., are all natural behaviours.

Natural instincts and behaviours should be nurtured in order to keep control of them and to be able to produce them on cue when they are needed. There are some natural instincts we may want to suppress as they are often not deemed to be socially acceptable to us, as with scent-marking their territory for example, or humping people or dogs for that matter.

My methodology

The method behind my training is, to begin with the natural instincts first and mark each one until the dog knows they are a good thing. How do we 'mark' a behaviour? You can either mark a behaviour with a clicker or with a word or sound.

For the purpose of my training I am going to use a word as this is my preferred method, if you would prefer to use a clicker, then you will need to purchase a clicker and buy a book or DVD and learn the theory and method before commencing it. I cannot tell you how many times I see a clicker being used incorrectly and they wonder why the dog isn't responding, please do your homework before trying to teach clicker.

How to mark a behaviour you that you want.

Let us start with some basic building blocks a **sit, down** and **stand**, these are positions your pup does many times in a day, so there is ample opportunity to mark these as behaviours from the day your puppy enters your home.

Step 1. Have some dog treats in your pocket or in a tub, watch your puppy and when she SITS, say "YES" and reward her with a food treat.

Repeat the same step for DOWN and STAND. She must only hear the word 'YES', when she has adopted the position.

Mr Tibs' Training Tip

It is very important to remember these steps. To help remember them, you could put them on post it notes and put them up where you and your family can see them and read them, making sure you all say the same words.

The YES word is your marker.

YES, tells your dog what it is you want her to do and that a tasty treat will be given every time she hears the word. The treat is your reinforcer.

You need to practice getting your timing right on the word so that you don't mark the wrong behaviour.

You must always offer a treat if you say the word YES, even if you made a mistake. Practice makes perfect.

Step 2. To help your dog understand what the name for the position she is doing is, we are going to add the word in front of the YES, so now when puppy sits, you are going to say "SIT, YES" and then reward. In a very short time the puppy will associate the position it is in with the word you have given it. It takes only a few repetitions of 'reward for action' before the dog will gladly repeat what you are asking her to do.

The word-association game

The word association game is basically say what you see, it she sits, say 'sit', if she downs, say 'down' etc. It's that simple for this early stage in training. This is the easiest way to have your dog learn to respond to instructions first time, such as Sit, Down, Stand, Come etc., by giving her the word as she is actually doing it. She should hear the word once only as she adopts the position. It won't take long before she makes the connection that putting her bottom to the floor is a 'sit', and then you can start to bring forward the word, i.e. give the word before she sits, so that she learns to sit when she hears the word the first time.

The following are some of the basic cue words and phrases that make up the building blocks for all future training, these exercises can all be taught now before your puppy has completed her vaccination program, so let's get going and create that super pup. Your trainer will be most impressed when you turn up to puppy class with a puppy who knows so much at such a young age.

The basic building blocks in training

Sit, Stand, Down, and Come are your basic building blocks. We will also look at the basics of lead walking.

Sit – why do we teach a dog to sit? Sit makes your dog easier to control, for example, putting the lead on and generally helps create good manners. Even if you are going to show your puppy, he can still learn 'Sit', they are very clever and they will know the difference between sit and stand, as long as you make the cue 'Stand' as important as the cue 'Sit'.

Step 1: With some tasty treats, chopped up small. Get your pup interested in the food in your hand and allow him to nibble at it. [See Photo 1]

Photo 1

Step 2. Slowly and steadily lift your hand upwards letting the pup lick at the food in your hand. As your pup looks upwards move your hand slightly over his head and his bottom will start to tilt towards the floor, it is an automatic reaction, head goes up, and bottom goes down. [See Photo 2]

Photo 2

Step 3: As your pup's bottom touches the floor say, 'Yes' 'Good Girl' and then reinforce the position with the treat. [Photo 3]

Repeat steps 1 to 3 a number of times, your pup will soon realise that when she puts her bottom on the floor, she gets a treat. You will find every time she appears in front of you she sits expectantly.

Photo 3

Without realising it your puppy is learning a hand signal for 'sit' as well as the verbal cue. The hand signal is your hand held out above her, with your open palm facing towards you.

Over time, you can work toward reducing the treats to random rewarding, although don't do it too soon as your puppy won't see the point in working for nothing. Your puppy must always hear verbal praise from you if she is to keep motivated and work, otherwise she will give up as there is nothing in it for her.

Step 4: Once your pup is responding consistently, by sitting when your hand goes up, you can introduce the cue word 'Sit'. She must only hear the word as she does the action. I.e. The pup's bottom touches the floor and you say 'Sit, Yes'.

Stand - Why teach a 'Stand'?
Stand is very useful, but for many pet owners it is the least taught. It is essential if you are considering entering your pup into breed showing.

It is useful to have a dog that can stand when a vet needs to examine them. It is important for long-haired dogs, to stay standing to make the job easier when grooming them, particularly if they are going to have to visit a grooming salon regularly. It is also very useful when the ground is wet and you don't want her to sit at the road-side, so she doesn't get a wet bottom!

o   Now your puppy has learned to sit it makes it easier to teach the stand.

Step 1:

With your puppy in a sit take a treat to her mouth, making sure your hand does not go above the dog's eye-level as it did with the sit, she needs to be looking straight ahead to achieve the stand, remember when the head goes up bottom goes down, so we want her looking forward. [Photo 4]

Photo 4

Step 2:

With your puppy nibbling on the treat, pull your hand back slowly away from the puppy her and let her follow the treat you are holding, take it very slowly, as she needs to keep contact with the food to keep her attention. [Photo 5]

Photo 5

Step 3:

As soon as your puppy is on her feet reinforce the behaviour with the, 'Yes', Good Girl and release the food at the same time, to reinforce what she has just done. Remember food should be your secondary reinforcer, 'you' should be the primary reinforcer by verbally rewarding her, so that it isn't just about the food.

Step 4:

Once the puppy is following the food consistently you can start asking her to hold still, once she is on her feet. While your puppy is busy trying to get her piece of food introduce the cue word 'Stand, Yes'. Once your puppy starts to grasp this gently tickle her tummy to encourage her to keep standing. She will soon be standing like a pro.

Remember keep your sessions short, only 5 to 10 repetitions to keep your pup's interest and do not tire her out.

Down – Why teach a down?

The down is a very important position for your dog to learn. The down can be used as an emergency position to stop your dog getting into trouble. The down is the ultimate control position necessary to ensure your dog stays calm.

Step 1:

Following the same procedure as with the sit and stand, get your piece of food and encourage your puppy into the sit, let her nibble at the food and move your hand in a straight line from her chin to the floor, as close to her paws as possible.

Step 2:

Move slowly as though puppy is attached to your hand, giving her time to follow. [See

Photo 6

Photo 6] If you move too quickly she will remain sitting, if you move your hand forward instead of in a straight line to the ground, she will stand up. Once your hand reaches the floor, keep it still on the ground, puppy will be constantly licking and trying to retrieve the piece of food from you, do not let go of it until she is fully lying down on the floor.

A few repetitions and it will click with the puppy that when she lies down you release the food. Once puppy is fully in a down, mark the position with 'Yes', 'Good Girl', at the same time reinforcing the position by releasing the food. [Photo 7]

Photo 7

111

Once your puppy is following your hand consistently to the floor introduce the cue 'Down', before the 'Yes'. Given time she will build up the association of the action with the cue.

In order to repeat the exercise, simply use a treat while your puppy is in the down and start to slowly raise your hand from the floor, your puppy will follow your hand with the treat stretching upwards and eventually bring herself back to a sit, as she does it give the cue 'Sit', 'Yes' 'Good Girl', and release the food to her. [Photo 8]

Photo 8

She has now learned to sit from a down, and you are now ready to practice the down again.

Mr Tibs' Training Tips

- *Keep the training sessions short.*
- *Keep them fun.*
- *Give lots of praise when your puppy does what you want her to do and do not comment or reprimand if she gets it wrong.*
- *Aim to have your training sessions before her meal times so that your puppy isn't tired and is interested in food treats.*
- *If neither of you are in the mood, play instead; and always set yourself and your puppy up to succeed - take little steps that you know you can achieve and always end on a good note, then you will both look forward to training sessions!*

Total 'Recall' through play

What is a recall? A recall is the term used in dog training to describe getting your dog to come to you. Basically it is calling your dog to come to you.

It is essential for all dogs to learn a recall and the earlier they learn it the better. It is also quite detailed, hence the length of this section as I felt I needed to do it justice making sure nothing is left out and to give you various methods that can all be used to enhance your recall. Some breeds are more difficult to recall than others. Hounds are often difficult due to their desire to follow their nose. Tibetan Terriers can be difficult, due to their independence although I have only experienced it with my first Tibetan because I didn't know how to make myself more important to him. I have never had a problem since.

I whistle train my litters to learn that whistle means food, I start this from the moment I start weaning. This way when I send each puppy home to their new owners with their whistle, the owner is already well on their way to having the perfect recall, if they keep up the work that I have started.

Puppies have a natural following instinct up until a certain age, this can vary from dog to dog depending on that dog's personality and its growth development. It is important that you build on this natural instinct while your puppy wants to be with you. As a puppy grows in confidence they will stray further and further from you and become more independent if you don't work with them. This period of Pre-Vaccination is a perfect time to establish a solid recall.

Whistle training for emergency Recalls
This is so simple to teach; every puppy should be taught it. What you need is a whistle the Acme 210.5 or 211 is the one I use.

How to whistle train your pup

Step 1:
The whistle will be used at meal times 'only' to begin with. Every meal you present to your pup; you will blow the whistle before offering her the food. I use two short blasts on it each time.

It doesn't matter how you decide to blow it, but it must be the same every time. You don't need to do anything else other than blow the whistle before every meal. This will build up a whistle = food,

113

association for your pup, it will take no time at all before she firmly believes that, every time she hears your whistle, food will follow.

Step 2:
You are not going to blow the whistle every time you want your dog to come, as she will get bored with it and it will become over used and loose its value.

I use the whistle for when my dog has gone perhaps too far from me or is playing with other dogs and I really need them to come to me now. I treat it as an emergency back up and this is what makes it very important to them that they respond to it. I always reward a bit extra in treat size when they respond to it and they know that, which makes it a much more reliable tool.

Recall training your puppy through play

WEEK1. This exercise should happen from day one of your puppy entering your home and should happen at different intervals throughout the day for the first week. This exercise teaches your puppy that following you is good fun and at the same time she will learn her name.

- Toilet your puppy, before beginning the exercise, so that she is not distracted.
- Arm yourself with a 10 to 15 high value treats, ready to pay your dog when she makes contact with you. Something that smells particularly strong is a good place to start with treats.
- Experiment with what makes her more excited. Cheese, liver or sausage etc.
- While your pup is very young, start by simply wandering around your garden and encourage her to follow you while occasionally saying her name. [photo 9]

Photo 9

- As she is catching up with you stop and turn to greet her with praise and a treat. Start again and keep it at a steady pace, and fun. Not too fast that she can't catch you, she will be uncoordinated at this age. Too slow and she will become more interested in what's on the ground, too fast and she will tire out very quickly.

As your puppy catches up with you, she may get over excited and jump up, this is your ideal opportunity to teach her to keep her feet on the floor, never reward the jumping up.

Simply. take the food lower to the ground and use the cue 'Off' while encouraging her to put her feet on the floor. As soon as she makes contact with the floor mark the behaviour with the 'Yes' word to identify what it is you want and then reinforce it with a food treat. [Photo 10]

Photo 10

WEEK 2 - 9 weeks of age, your puppy should have had a week to settle with you. Your puppy should now be aware of following you as in the previous exercise and now know her name.

Puppy-in-the-middle

You need at least two people to play this game, the purpose of the game is get your pup to run between two people when she hears her name.

If there are more than two family members, start with two until your puppy understands it and then add a third person in, alternatively alternate which two people get to play the game.

This is a great game for the children to get involved with but you must keep control of it so that the puppy doesn't get confused and give up.

Remember pups tire very quickly, so play must stop once all the food is gone.

STEP1. Start in one room of your house, with 2 people, both should have treats 5 to 10 small pieces, each person in turn calls the puppy to them:

- Cue – 'Puppy's name first, this should get her attention and she will turn and look at you. Come down to your pup's level.
- Hold your hand out with the treat in it, encouraging her to come to you.
- As she starts moving towards you, introduce the word 'Come' in an exciting tone, encouraging her all the way to you.
- When she reaches you, mark the behaviour with 'Yes' and reward her with the treat to reinforce it. DO NOT ask her to sit at this stage, for three reasons:

1. This would slow down her coming to you, as she anticipates having to do a sit.
2. It also makes the game boring for the dog if she has to keep sitting each time she comes.
3. She will enjoy it much more if she gets to run to you at speed. The reward she receives should be for coming to you not for sitting. If you want her to learn to sit at the end of coming to you, reward her first for coming, then ask for a sit and reward the sit, this way she gets two rewards.

Take her to different rooms in the house and practice the same exercise, perhaps the living room, the kitchen and the hall.

Mr Tibs' Training Tip

Step 1. Should be played two or three times a day for 1 week, before you move on to step 2.

Week 3. At 10 weeks of age your puppy should be quite proficient at coming galloping back and forwards when called between the two of you. It is time to move to the next step.

Step 2. Now your puppy is returning instantly between the two of you, increase the distance, perhaps have puppy come from room to room, increase the distance slowly and perhaps start by peeping round door, so that she knows where you are. Be patient and help her if she can't work it out. Her desire to find you and get her reward will soon spare her on. Practice calling her into different rooms.

NOTE: At no time must you call her and not reward her with a treat. Puppies loose interest very quickly and it won't take long for her to not see the point of the game if this happens.

Mr Tibs' Training Tip

Practice step 2 for 1 week, before progressing to step 3.

Week 4. At 11 weeks of age. Your puppy's recall should be flawless before moving onto Step 4. Spend an extra week working on step 2, if there is any doubt in your puppy's response.

Step 3. Now that your puppy can recall without seeing who is calling her, you can practice the same exercise in the garden, where the distractions are much greater.

- You have the sights, sounds and smells to compete with.
- You must make yourself more interesting and exciting than the world around her.
- You are going to go back and practice step 1 in the garden, to teach her that she should respond the same way in every environment and situation. Practice every day at least twice a day for 1 week.
- You can then practice recalling her from the garden back into the house, make sure someone can see your puppy at all times if you go back into the house to call her.

Do not leave her unattended in the garden she is far too young and accidents happen in a split-second.

Week 5. At 12 weeks. Your puppy should just about be ready to enter the world on her own four paws.

Step 4. Once your puppy has achieved Step 3 and is 100% reliable from the garden, you can then begin to teach 'Puppy-in-the-middle' in your local park, assuming the vaccination programme is complete.

- You will need to go back to step 1 again and practice calling her from person to person to remind her, what it is she is meant to do.
- I would highly recommend that you use a long flat training line in the park for safety reasons, until your puppy is reliable and big enough to cope with the advances of other dogs, the line also means you can guide your puppy if she gets it wrong with distractions, sights and sounds.

Ace's Top Tip

Your pup won't naturally transfer what she has learned indoors to the outdoors. You will need to teach her, that what she learns in each game applies in all situations. She will however, learn it faster as she already understands it.

Lead walking – who is leading who?

This is probably the one exercise that people do most with their dog and yet the one they have least success with.

We've all seen the familiar sight of owners having their arms stretched as they are walked by their dogs. Pulling on a lead is a learnt behaviour.

When owners first take their puppy out on a lead, it goes something like this:

o The puppy gallops along in front chasing everything in it's path or drags along behind planting her bottom firmly on the ground in protest.

o At this stage, the new owner really doesn't mind as puppy is happy exploring her new environment or they are all forgiving because puppy is scared or unsure.

o Here begins a long road of being dragged along behind your dog, or being prevented from going forward as your dog puts the breaks on to control where they want to go, as she grows up and leads the way on her walks.

The team leader should be leading the walk and the leader is you! Start as you mean to go on, it is so much easier to teach a tiny pup where you want it to walk than a 40kg dog, or even a 10 kg dog.

• Introduce your puppy to the collar as soon as you get her, I always put a collar on the day I collect my puppy. They are so busy dealing with everything that's new they barely notice they have one on.

• I find it best to put the collar on and leave it on and puppy will get used to it much quicker than if you keep putting it on and off. The litters I have bred, all have collars fitted from 6 weeks old and completely forget about them within 1 day.

• For safety reasons make sure the collar fits snuggly allowing just two fingers to slide under it. If the collar is too loose, this can prove hazardous for the puppy. When the collar fits snuggly, this ensures that your pup cannot get her collar caught on anything, remember to check the tension on the collar as your pup is growing all the time.

Important safety measure: *it is a good idea to remove the collar before your pup into her crate to sleep, if you are leaving them or at bedtime.*

If your puppy has already been with you a few days, she will probably object when the collar goes on, she may dart about like a mad thing, and roll around the floor scratching at herself as though she is being eaten by giant fleas, she may even cry.

Do not worry or panic! Simply, make sure that you have some tasty treats at hand, and distract her. Try to encourage her to work with you by offering her food. It often helps to take them out in the garden, where there is more to take their mind of it outside.

- Puppies move on very quickly; lots of play will also take her mind of it. Once your pup is used to the collar, attaching the lead will be much easier. Make sure she is completely happy with the collar before starting lead walking.
- Encourage your pup to follow you using lots of praise and encouragement. If she pulls backwards against you just stand still and wait. She may object strongly, thrashing about, do not correct her, just ignore it. It will be short lived and she will give in when she realises she has to go with you in your direction.
- Once your pup is happy on the lead, she will start trying to go ahead of you, this is when you must take charge so that she doesn't develop bad habits like pulling. Remember, you have a puppy on a lead, so don't use sharp jerks to correct her.
- Start by standing still and wait to see what she does. If she gets very agitated try encouraging her to come back to you, then relax the lead and start to walk forward when she is beside you.

Another method that may help your puppy

- When your puppy reaches the end of the lead, turn and walk away from her, she will have no option but to turn and play catch up with you.
- As soon as she reaches you praise and reward her.
- As soon as she starts to get ahead of you turn away again and keep walking until she catches up.
- Keep repeating the action until she learns that she needs to pay attention or you will move away from her. Reward her every time she joins you.

It is so important to establish where and how your puppy should be walking before she goes out in the great big world.

Mr Tibs' Training Tip

When teaching lead work, do not set off through your door to leave your house, while your puppy is excited and jumping around, as this will set the tone of your walk, which may be quite manic. Wait until puppy is calm and then exit the house.

14 Learning to Play with your Dog

In this chapter

Food vs toy training

Sometimes people are unsure whether they should train using food or a toy, many owners are unaware that using a toy for training their dog is even possible. This is purely down to your preference and which your dog responds best to. Some dogs are not interested in toys and although it is possible to teach them to play, if you are a beginner dog owner/trainer will find it much easier to gain a response from your dog using food.

- To train with a toy, you need a dog that is very toy orientated in order for the toy to work; this can be achieved by playing regularly with your dog with a special toy. Choose a toy that your dog seems to like to get hold of.
- The toy should be brought out specifically for your play together and put away after the end of your session, this way the dog will look forward to your sessions together with her special toy.
- Training with a toy can be slower as the dog needs sometime to play with the toy, to see it as a reward. Teaching exercises may take a little more time, but it is very rewarding once achieved.
- It is a good idea to incorporate both a toy and food into your training sessions, this provides your dog with the best of both worlds.

If using food, you will see very fast results, but the real skill in using food is in getting the dog to complete the exercises without having food in your hands. This will come through time, experience and learning to do the weaning process from the treats.

What is a good dog treat?

Not just any old treat will do, particularly in the early stages of training. To get the best from your dog, i.e. Attention and keenness, you need to learn what really matters to your dog and pay her well.

What you would like to feed your dog as a treat and what your dog may choose as a treat could be at opposite ends of the pole. Anyone who has ever trained with me will know that I am very specific about what treats they should bring to the class.

Treats SHOULD be something soft. (The dog can choke very easily when excited during training, as they tend to swallow quickly, rather than chew their food).

Treats SHOULD be something, which can be chopped very small (The idea is not to fill the dog but to leave her wanting more.)

Treats SHOULD be something your dog would consider a 'real treat', and not something he gets every day. What your dog considers a treat in the house or garden may not be exciting enough for him when outdoors in a park or in a training room full of other dogs.

Treats SHOULD be something your dog considers of value, and will work hard to get. What you consider high value your dog may not agree.

I consider the value of a treat as payment, you wouldn't work for free and neither should your dog have to. Be prepared to pay up if you want to get the best from your dog.

High value treats
- Cheese
- Sausage - (or similar type of meat chopped very small.)
- Frankfurter
- Ham
- Cooked Chicken - (In small amounts. Too much protein will give Tibetan Terriers and upset tummy and may do the same for other dogs).

- Liver (the ultimate delicacy, when all else fails with fussy dogs, bring out the liver, but be careful it is very rich and can give the runs, mixing some pieces of liver in a bag with other less valuable treats may do the trick).

Low Value Treats
- Dog Biscuits (too hard, too big)
- *Bonios* (too hard, too big.)
- Puppy Treats (are ok for occasional short training sessions at home, but not in a training class, due to the high volume that need to be fed, your puppy is likely to have an upset tummy if fed what is needed in school and is likely to cough them back up).
- Dog Meal – (she sees dog meal every day, working for it will not be high on the list of exciting treats).

Pay-up and pay-well

When you are going to ask your dog to work for you at any time, remind yourself of this statement. "If I am to expect the best from my dog, then it is only fair that I offer her the best reward I can".

As dogs are carnivorous then for most, meat will be their ultimate choice. (no matter what you think) Although in the wild they will also eat berry's and grasses etc., but they must have meat to survive and they certainly won't choose a berry over meat if given a choice.

Dogs are not vegetarian so whatever your personal preference is for your own diet; do not try to inflict this on your dog. Although your dog may enjoy indulging in some of what you want her to eat at home, when you are faced with a class of other dogs and exciting smells of tasty treats, you will need to compete for your dog's attention. Experiment with what your dog considers worth working for, carrot won't compete with liver or sausage.

Having experimented to some degree with other people, their dogs and treat preferences, the response to training (particularly with the recall) was far higher in the dogs fed some form of meat as a treat. A lot of owners found that the biscuits and puppy treats were fine within the confines of the house and in their garden, but beyond the home, meat treats had a far greater attraction, with the occasional dog going crazy for some cheese, but again be careful of volume.

Which games are the right games?

All dogs naturally play with each other; they learn their skills for life through play. Over the years selective breeding has accentuated certain traits in certain breeds. E.g. Sheepdogs (the Herding instinct), Guarding Dogs (Protection), Terriers (digging). Sometimes these traits can make living with the family pet a problem, which is why we need to channel these traits into something constructive rather than try to get rid of them. That way we can have a better and more enjoyable relationship with our dogs.

We all know that we need to exercise our dogs physically however, this alone is not enough; dogs also need mental stimulus to keep them satisfied. This is achieved through training and through play sessions. Your dog can learn the good and bad behaviour through the games you play with her.

How to play with your dog

Playing the right games with your pup are essential for bonding with her and for her development. Playing the wrong games can set behaviours in motion, that you may not even be aware are developing. Puppies learn most of their life skills through playing, they learn how to hunt, how hard they need to bite to restrain their prey, who is the strongest, when to submit etc. Therefore, the games you choose to play with your dog can influence their relationship with you.

Play is not just a matter of taking your dog off-lead and letting her run free. The play we are talking about here is an interaction between you as the handler or leader and your dog. The games you play with your dog will affect her attitude to you later in life.

Tug-o-War

This game is frowned upon by many as a game of strength and dominance, however I personally view this game as a wonderful exercise for allowing you and your dog to get to know one another, she  will learn your strengths and hopefully you won't reveal your weaknesses through playing it. Tug-o-war allows your dog to learn respect for you and any item you share with her.

When you play Tug-O-War do not let your pup wonder off with the toy as each time she achieves this she may consider herself as having won the challenge. Attach a lead or indoor puppy training line to your puppy's collar, to prevent her from running off when she decides to end the game.

Tug-o-war is a great game for teaching your puppy she must let go when you tell her and that she can only play the game if she plays by your rules. You should teach her she can only bite the toy when you tell her to get it and release it when she hears the release cue 'Off' or 'Leave It'.

When you decide the game is over, stop it and end by keeping possession of the toy and putting it away where the dog cannot get to it until the next time you decide to play again, that way you have taught her, that the toy is yours and that you will invite her to share it with you, but you are the game keeper and you set the rules of the game.

When your pup is biting on the toy, often they work their way up the toy to take hold of the end you are holding. Do not allow this; stop the game by removing the toy from puppy and allowing him only to have the end you have decided. If you allow him to swap to the end you are holding he will believe he is in control of the game.

Mr Tibs' Training Tip

All games must be played to your rules. You must be able to stop the game and take possession of the toy when you choose to do so.

Chase games

Running with the puppy around the garden, is another favourite past time that people seem to take great pleasure in playing with the dog. This is fun until the sheepdog or the terrier puppy starts to grow and is nipping at your ankles or the German Shepherd Puppy leaps to knock you down, then the fun ends and now we have a problem. Puppies may not run very fast, but it doesn't take long for them to master the art of beating you at this game. You will never win in a game of chase against your dog. They are always going to catch you or learn to avoid you.

Teaching your dog how to outwit you in the chase games means she learns how to avoid you whenever it might be essential that you get hold of her. My dogs have no concept of what it means to run away from me as in their world coming to me is always the better option and is always rewarding.

Ace's Top Tips

NEVER chase after your dog when she picks something up that she should not have. This will only encourage your dog to run away from you and will cause you problems later on. You will never win a game of chase. From a young age your puppy will be a master at it and win every time.

Go away from her if she is running round the garden refusing to be caught, even hide from her. Trust me curiosity 'might kill the cat', but curiosity will cure the dog, it will get the better of her and she

127

will come looking for you, it is our desire to be with you not to be alone.

Practice rewarding her for giving things to you or letting you take them and in case you are thinking it, 'no she won't start stealing so that you'll reward her'.

Far better to have your dog give things to you, than for her to chew them or even worse swallow them.

Which toys are good toys?

The toy market is incredible now days for dogs, it is never ending in the types of toys that are available for the pleasure of you and your dog to enjoy together. Some are good and some are not so good and many are very expensive. Look for the indestructible ones, as these are the safest for your dog to be left with however I don't have one dog who will lie and chew on hard rubber, I guess it is trial and error to find their preference.

Most puppies love a fluffy toy, but as your pup grows and shows an interest in chewing, do not leave them alone with it, as for many shredding a soft fluffy quickly develops into a skill and digesting the innards of the toy, could have serious consequences.

Suitable toys include the Kong puppy range.

The Kongs shown here are a range of puppy toys suitable for approx. up to 9 months old.

Please note that these are by no means the only suitable toys, but they are a selection of safe and reliable toys. *Nylabone* also make a safe range of puppy toys.

Ace's Top Tip

Remember one size does not fit all. If you own a large breed puppy, make sure you pick toys that are suitable for their size, so that they can't choke on them.

The rubber on the puppy range is slightly softer than those used for the adult toys – to encourage your puppy to want to chew on them; they are made with teething in mind. These toys are designed to be stuffed or filled with treats, you can purchase specific fillings for them or you can make your own home made fillings for them.

You can purchase liver pate specially made for them, and various other fillings. These toys are also designed to be frozen with the filling in which gives a longer lasting experience for the dog.

If you are looking for a toy to throw, a ball on a rope toy is the safest as the dog cannot choke on it, but be careful you don't hit your dog, yourself or someone else with it, they are extremely hard as they are made to last.

Do Not Ever Throw sticks for your dog, they are so dangerous, ask any vet about the injury's they have seen with sticks and they will tell you many, many horrific stories.

In the photo my dog Amara is proudly showing off a stick that she found, she had never played with a stick in her life until this day and I have no idea what was so special about this stick that she found, but she spent the whole walk with it, carrying it and running with it, I did find highly

amusing and got some lovely photos of her with it, however, she has never played with a stick since, probably because I didn't engage with it with her, as I am all too aware of the dangers.

When you are at home with your dog and playing together, I find that home-made toys are very much my puppies favourites.

o   A ball inside a sock with a knot in the end.
o   A sock stuffed with newspapers with a knot tied at either end.
o   An empty pop bottle, obviously take the top of it first. (Do Not allow them to eat it, make sure you supervise their play times with it).

Make sure the chew you leave your puppy with is not one she can ingest. You should always be present if your dog is going to be given something to gnaw on. Sterile bones are great that you can stuff with your own ingredients, to keep your puppy busy for a while, although be careful what you use as a filler in the early days. Remember, eating leads to drinking which leads to weeing and pooing. This may be counterproductive to your toilet training. You will need to make a judgement call based on your individual puppy.

15 Play-biting or Mouthing

I decided to dedicate quite a large section to this subject, as it is the single biggest behaviour that causes every new puppy owner a problem. There are many methods for dealing with the biting puppy, some good and some not so good.

It's only natural

The first thing you should know about play biting or mouthing, whichever you prefer to call it is, it is normal. It is a natural behaviour for any puppy with other dogs, but it doesn't mean it's a good thing for a puppy to do with humans. Puppies are not being mean when they bite, they are merely doing what comes naturally and what they know. There are those who would argue that to stop puppies from biting altogether would be to deprive them of their natural behaviour or rights. In my opinion the only way to guarantee a dog never bites is to never encourage it to make contact with your skin.

Dogs mouth one another when playing, they learn how much pressure they are allowed to put on the other dog to keep control of the game, they learn when young that by putting too much bite pressure on, causes the other puppy to yelp and often the other puppy no longer wants to play. This means all fun may end, however by learning to keep control over how much pressure they exert the game may continue. (The term used to describe this is Bite Inhibition). However, my experience tells me this is not always the case. I have spent many hours watching puppies play in litters I have bred and in other litters I have been invited to observe, of many different breeds. I have observed on many occasions that the yelp and back off system, does not work for all dogs. Sensitive dogs are often responsive to this method, but there are many who are not, there are many who become quite charged up and almost excited when this happens and often they will bite harder. It is these puppies that many owners will struggle with if they opt for the teaching Bite inhibition.

In each of the litters that I have bred and observed, there has always been the exception to the rule, particularly as the puppies grew in age and strength. I would regularly observe a game getting out of hand where a puppy would be screaming as its ear, face or paw received bite pressure from another puppy, at no time would the biting puppy back off or let go for a second, in fact I have also experienced other puppies join in the frenzy and becoming quite excited by the commotion and attempt to bite the screaming puppy too. On many occasions I or the breeder have stepped in and intercepted such brawls, to teach the offending puppy this is not acceptable.

It is at this moment that I would like to point out to you, just in case you are not aware, 'you' are not a dog, you do not have to play with your dog the way she would with other dogs. You do not go around sniffing her butt, you do not feed at the same meal as her (well if you do perhaps you shouldn't be), therefore it is perfectly acceptable that your puppy learns the no bite, no contact via teeth with human skin rule. Let her save that behaviour for playing with her own kind and the toys and chews you provide her with.

No teeth contact rule

Allowing a puppy to mouth at your hands or fingers they quickly learn that by applying a certain amount of pressure she can make you with draw your hands from her. As the puppy gets older she will soon realise that she can use this game to stop you from grooming or handling her by using exactly the same behaviour. I exercise a complete 'NO BITE' rule with my dogs and in my training school. I teach puppies from very young that making contact with human skin is never acceptable. In my opinion this is the only way to remove from a dog's behavioural patterns the thought of ever lashing out and biting as being acceptable. I have practiced this method for many years now after exploring every other method that has come along, including bite inhibition etc. and while we can never guarantee 100% that a dog won't bite for me this has proven by far to be my most successful approach to teaching a puppy that teeth to skin contact is never acceptable. This also ensures that children don't accidentally get chomped on.

No contact with skin is so ingrained into my dogs that even in a game of tug-o-war with a toy if a tooth accidentally touches my hand they will instantly release the toy and stop until I have told them it's ok. Often this has happened and I was barely aware that they have touched me, they become so sensitive about the feel of skin to tooth contact. I love when my dog has made this connection that this is not a good thing. This is as close to guaranteeing 'No Bite' as it gets in my opinion.

Obviously for working dogs or therapy dogs, this method would need to be modified, but we are talking about pet dogs here, 'your dog'. Your dog and all pet dogs need to be safe around children and the elderly with their more delicate skin. Teaching the 'No Bite', method, brings you one step closer to providing a dog who knows how to play without using their mouth to gain control of the game.

There are however other thoughts on teaching different methods for puppies not to bite, I am going to look briefly at each of the most popular methods and give my opinion on them and explain a little about why I don't use them. You are however welcome to make your own decision on which method you would prefer to use. Remember, just because something is popular doesn't make it right.

Which method is right for you and your pup?
You will no doubt have read of many methods on how to deal with a puppy biting. I am going to highlight the 3 most common methods that people seem to try and give my opinions on them. Then I will give a 4th method, which is my preferred method.

Method 1: When the pup tries to bite you, your reaction needs to be quick in order to get a reaction from the pup, a sharp "Yip!" or "Ouch!" at the pup should hopefully make her stop playing and move away for a few seconds until she has calmed down. You should re-start the game as though nothing has happened. Always have a chew-toy at hand for your dog to chew on. You must teach your dog what she can and cannot chew on. Providing a chew-toy at the time, will help with this.

My Opinion: This method I find only works for some puppies not all, usually sensitive puppies will react to this as they are easily startled, however even sensitive puppies acclimatise to the noise and soon realise it means nothing and there is no consequence for the action. i.e. nothing bad happens, so they are safe to continue.

Method 2 When puppy bites get up and walk away, give puppy a couple of minutes to think about what happened and return to her when she has calmed down.

My Opinion: This method can back fire on you as the leader. Depending on why puppy is biting at the time (there can be a few reasons), she may feel she achieved exactly what she wanted which could be you to go away and leave her alone, depending on what you were doing at the time. She may see you're moving away as weak and a clear triumph for her.

Method 3 When puppy starts to bite or gets over excited, put her away in her crate or in another room for 5 minutes or so as a time out and then let her return to the room when she has calmed down.

My Opinion: I don't believe dogs do time out, this is a human concept. Over time of practicing this method, your puppy may start to regard, being put in another room or her crate, as a punishment and start refusing to go in to it, or even refuse to let you catch her to put her away, this exercise can very quickly become confrontational. There is no doubt that removing the dog from the situation stops it 'for that moment', and while some dogs may make the connection that the reason they have been put away is because their behaviour was unacceptable, my experience tells me that more dogs go straight back to the behaviour when the opportunity arises, and the cycle continues.

Method 4 The method I prefer to use for teaching puppies not to bite provides the puppy with a consequence for the action. Having tried and tested all the methods that are generally used, over many years, I have found when the puppy receives a consequence for the action she gives up much faster and generally thinks very carefully about whether to repeat the action.

I refer to this action as putting a block on the puppy, which teaches the puppy Bite Prohibition, rather than Bite Inhibition. It prevents her from being able to bite or continue the game. This method works best on young puppies, and needs to start from the moment puppy comes into your home, to teach them that mouth on skin is never acceptable, by the time your puppy is 12 to 14 weeks it may be too late to apply this method, depending on the pup.

Being prepared in play

As we have already established, while interacting with your puppy, it is safe to assume that at some point they are going to attempt biting, it goes with the territory of being a puppy, so it should be easy for you to remember and be prepared. Make sure you have toys and chew things to hand that your puppy likes to chew on. However there will always be that time when your puppy wants to chew only on you, and she seems completely disinterested in what else you have to offer. However, this behaviour usually happens with slightly older puppies, young puppies between 8 and 12 weeks are 'usually' easily distracted.

So with chew toys at the ready play time with your puppy can begin. If at any time your puppy changes their attention from the toy to your hands, you should:

- Take hold of her and keep hold until she stops struggling, you do not need to lift her off the floor, simply hold her where she is.
- Do not push her over onto her side or her back. This is not designed as a pin your puppy down exercise. You should never pin your puppy down. This can create a very untrusting puppy

135

who feels the need to become defensive over a position which should be relaxing, i.e. lying on their back or on their side.

- The best place to hold the puppy to put a block on is across their shoulders and chest, as though you are holding a rugby ball.

Holding the dog puts a block on them and freezes what they are doing, they don't like it because you are interfering with what they would prefer to do, once they give up the fight, you will find that just by touching them with one hand will be enough to dissuade them from putting their mouth on you. I cannot stress enough how important consistency is with this exercise. There must be no room for letting puppy get away with making mouth contact with your skin. It is your job and responsibility to create a socially acceptable pet who is reliable around strangers and reliable and trustworthy around children.

- As soon as she stops struggling and trying to bite, relax your hands on her and resume whatever you were doing before, direct her to a chew or toy, so that she knows what she is allowed to chew on. Praise her when she is chewing and playing with the right thing.
- Do not use your voice to reprimand her, this may frighten her. Let your hands be the signal that she needs, and they will do the talking.
- It is very, very important that as soon as your puppy directs their mouth towards your skin, your hands need to go on to her straight away and hold her firmly. This becomes the consequence for the action. Your hands are mimicking what your pup is doing to you.

Note: If you have practiced the restraint exercise in the handling and grooming section, this will make hands on for biting so much easier for your puppy to accept, as she will already be in the process of learning to respect you when you put your hands on her or hold her. However this exercise is not to be confused with the restraint. The restraint is a completely different exercise and at no time should it be used to stop your puppy from biting. The Restraint is not to be used as a correction it is purely for teaching puppy to relax for handling.

Do Not, play-wrestle your puppy with your hands or feet. She must never be encouraged to make contact with you with her teeth, even in play. This is very confusing for a dog and is counterproductive in trying to teach them NO BITE.

It is very confusing for the dog when the dad at home play wrestles with the dog, because his hands can take it, but then the dog is suddenly stopped for trying the same game with mum or the children. It is unfair for the dog to have to understand that sometimes the biting rule is ok and other times not. The NO BITE rule keeps your children safe, teaching bite inhibition does not.

16 The Journey Begins

This is the start of your journey through one of the greatest relationships you will ever have. It is my hope that you embrace and enjoy all that your dog has to offer you and that you remember daily that as with any relationship it is a two-way street, it is equally important that you give of yourself to your dog, and meet her daily needs, if you are to expect to receive in return from her.

Any good relationship is built on trust, understanding, love, friendship and teamwork. I hope you enjoy your journey, in developing your relationship with your dog, as much as I have with mine. I am so grateful for all that the dogs in my life have taught me. I am always regretful for the mistakes that I have made with each dog I have shared my life with, but the lesson I hope I learn, is to not repeat the same mistake. Learn from your mistakes, it is what will make you a great dog trainer and a quality leader and companion to your' dog.

So your puppy is now approximately 12 weeks old and is fully vaccinated. Your journey together should be less bumpy now, if you have implemented what you have read.

Your first hurdle is complete but my suggestion to you, is that you go back to the beginning of this book and read again the section on understanding your dog.

Remind yourself what it is that makes your pup tick, why she does the things she does and keep reminding yourself to strive to understand her better. If she is getting it wrong and not doing what you ask her, always examine yourself first, ask yourself:
- Have you actually taught her what it is you are asking of her?
- Does she really understand what you are saying? Assume she does not, give her the benefit of the doubt and help her.
- Do not see her as out to get you, or as doing things deliberately to wind you up or to make you angry. She has no concept of such behaviour, she is a dog, such behaviours are human traits.

You are about to unleash the big wide world on your puppy with all that it has to offer her, in her journey through puppyhood and adolescents. It is your job and responsibility to help her grow and achieve her full potential as a socially acceptable dog. Dogs are like any good investment; you will only get out what you put in.

A dog never stops learning throughout their life. The sad part is that most people stop teaching them or working with them by the time they are a year or two years old. Dogs go through constant changes in their development until approximately 4 years old. I often get calls from people saying the dog has suddenly started crying when left alone, or it is digging or chewing and barking at strangers. You will have missed the signs that your dog was telling you, they need more. They are growing up and have other needs that need met. It seldom if ever 'just suddenly happens', you just didn't read the signs.

Your dog should be a pleasure to take out in your community, a friend to your family and playmate to the dogs in the park. It is your job to help her achieve this.

There will be events and moments in her development that prove challenging for both of you. Remember she cannot achieve her full potential without you. You are her leader and her guide through everything that she faces. She did not ask to be born and she did not ask to be yours, 'you choose her', stand by her and see her mistakes as your own and learn from them. Help her to get it right and be the best she can possibly be, this is the greatest gift you can give your puppy. Thank you for joining in with 'Pre-Vaccination Puppy Training'. Please spread the word so that other puppies can reach their full potential in a stress free environment.

If you would like to contact me to let me know how this book worked for you and your puppy, or if you would be interested in booking me for a seminar or training workshop, please email me at **julie@acek9.net**.

Also by Julie Hindle on amazon

Separation Anxiety is one of the most common canine behavioural disorders, it leads to many dogs ending up in rescue centres or even being euthanised. However, the good news is, it is also highly treatable.

If you have a dog suffering with separation anxiety, this book will give you the hands-on tools you need to understand and cope with it, by giving you a step-by-step guide to solving or preventing your dog being stressed.

The methods given in this book, are based on Julie's thirty-years' experience as a dog trainer and applied canine behaviourist.

Top amazon reviews

⭐⭐⭐⭐⭐ **An excellent read**
I loved reading this book, I gave it full rating because it offers hope, vast knowledge, simplicity to correct and humour.

⭐⭐⭐⭐⭐ **A must for all prospective dog owners**
Unlike many current dog behaviour books which are written by people with theory but no practical experience, this one has been written by someone with a wealth of hands on experience of dogs.

⭐⭐⭐⭐⭐ **A fascinating insight into dog behaviour**
I have had dogs all my life and got into breeding and showing dogs just over 20 years ago. There are ideas in here that never occurred to me and that have helped my puppy buyers tremendously. Great little book. A must have for puppy buyers.

Made in the USA
Las Vegas, NV
29 December 2020